Table of Contents

Ronald Labonte is Canada Research Chair in Globalization/Health Equity at the Institute of Population Health, University of Ottawa. A public health sociologist by predilection, he accrued 15 years of government service and 10 years work as an international consultant in health promotion and community empowerment before joining academia full-time in 1999. He is a founding member of the Canadian Coalition for Global Health Research, a past board member of local, provincial, national and international health associations in Canada, and a member of the Peoples' Health Movement.
E-mail: rlabonte@uottawa.ca

Ted Schrecker is a senior policy researcher at the Institute of Population Health, University of Ottawa. A political scientist by background, he has more than 20 years of professional experience as a legislative researcher, consultant and academic. His special interests are in issues at the interface of science, ethics, law and public policy and in causal pathways that link globalization with domestic social and economic policy by way of changes in class structure and class allegiances.
E-mail: tschrecker@sympatico.ca

Amit Sen Gupta trained in medicine and works on issues related to public health and pharmaceuticals policy, on which he has lectured and written extensively. He is also involved in implementing rural industrialization programs in India through the Centre for Technology and Development, is Secretary of the All India Peoples Science Network, and co-convenor of the Peoples' Health Movement (India) and member of the Movement's International Steering Group.
E-mail:ctddsf@vsnl.com

Acknowledgments

This short book is part of an ongoing program of research that could not have been carried out without the research assistance of Helen Oliver, Kyla Avis, Madeline Johnson, Jennifer Rodenbush, Renee Torgerson and Jennifer Cushon. The authors acknowledge with thanks the comments of anonymous external reviewers with the Global Health Watch project, and of Lisa Forman, David Zakus, David Woodward and John Hilary on earlier drafts. Editorial suggestions by Jane Salvage, David McCoy and Mike Rowson were also appreciated.
All views expressed are exclusively those of the authors.

Prologue

The current path of globalization must change. Too few share in its benefits. Too many have no voice in its design and no influence in its course. (World Commission on the Social Dimensions of Globalization [subsequently cited as WCSDG] 2004: 2)

In rural China, high school student Zheng Qingming kills himself by jumping in front of a train. Friends say it was because he couldn't afford the last US$ 80 of school tuition fees, which meant he could not take the college admission test. The overall annual tuition is more than the average village family in his region earns in a year. Health care, like education, has become scarce and expensive since China embraced the market economy, and his grandfather had already spent the family savings on treating a lung disease.

In Zambia, Chileshe waits painfully to die from AIDS. The global funds and antiretroviral programmes are too little and too late for her. She was infected by her now dead husband, who once worked in a textile plant along with thousands of others but lost his job when Zambia opened its borders to cheap, second-hand clothing. He moved to the city as a street vendor, selling cast-offs or donations from wealthier countries. He would get drunk and trade money for sex – often with women whose own husbands were somewhere else working, or dead, and who themselves desperately needed money for their children. Desperation, she thought, is what makes this disease move so swiftly; she recalls that a woman from Zaire (now the Democratic Republic of the Congo) passing through her village once said that the true meaning of SIDA, the French acronym for AIDS, was "Salaire Insuffisant Depuis des Années" – too little money for too many years (as documented by Schoepf 1998).

In northern Mexico, a young girl named Antonia is suffering from severe asthma. She is falling far behind in school. Her parents don't have enough money to pay for specialists or medicines, and wonder whether her problems are connected to the industrial haze and foul-smelling water that come from the nearby factory. They can't afford to move. All their savings were used up when corn prices plunged after the border opened to imports from the US, and it is not clear how they would make a living. How could so much corn grow so cheaply, her father Miguel used to wonder.

In a Canadian suburb, two people die when a delivery van swerves into oncoming traffic and slams into their car. The van driver, Tom, survives. He either fell asleep at the wheel or suffered a mild heart attack. No one knows, and he cannot remember. It was his 15th day of work without a rest. When the assembly plant where he once worked relocated to Mexico, driving the van became one of his three part-time jobs, at just over minimum wage and with no benefits. He alternated afternoon shifts at two fast food outlets, did early night shifts at a gas station and drove the van late nights as often as the company needed him. With the recession over, they had needed him a lot lately.

Health for Some:

*Death, Disease and Disparity
in a Globalizing Era*

Ronald Labonte

Ted Schrecker

Amit Sen Gupta

Centre for Social Justice
Toronto

Library and Archives Canada Cataloguing in Publication Data

Labonté, Ronald N.
Health for some : death, disease and disparity in a globalizing era
    Ronald Labonte, Ted Schrecker, Amit Sen Gupta.
Includes bibliographical references and index.
ISBN 0-9733292-3-8

1. Globalization--Health aspects. 2. World health. 3. Medical policy--
International cooperation. I. Schrecker, Ted II. Sen Gupta, Amit
III. Centre for Social Justice IV. Title.

RA425.L23 2005   362.1'042
C2005-902772-X

Published by Centre for Social Justice
489 College Street, Suite 303, Toronto, ON M6G 1A5
Ph: 416-927-0777   Toll Free: 1-888-803-8881
Fax: 416-927-7771
Email: justice@socialjustice.org
www.socialjustice.org

Date of publication – 2005
Printed and bound in Canada by union labour
Photo of India used in cover photo-collage - © Joerg Boethling / GlobalAware

Layout and Cover Design:
Visualeyez CREATIVE • Alan Pinn
Email: alanpinn@cogeco.ca • 705.741.4729

1 Introduction

These vignettes show how recent, rapid changes in our global economy can imperil the health of millions. The first describes a real event.[1] The other three are composites, like those used in the World Bank's *World Development Report 1995* (World Bank 1995), but in this case based on evidence that the remarkable accumulation of wealth associated with transnational economic integration ('globalization') has deepened the division between the rich and the rest, with serious adverse consequences for population health.

Winners from globalization, in high- and low-income countries alike, comprise a global elite that sociologist Zygmut Bauman (1998) calls "tourists." They have the money and status to "move through the world" motivated only by their dreams and desires. "Vagabonds," on the other hand, are those less privileged hundreds of millions whose migrations to escape war, famine or poverty, or to pursue opportunity and a better life are not welcome: North Africans crossing the Mediterranean, Chinese hiding in Canadian-bound cargo ships, and more than a million Mexicans each year who try unsuccessfully to enter the United States illegally. National borders are increasingly closed to them. Not all of globalization's losers become vagabonds, but their numbers may continue to rise as losers outnumber winners, because of how winners have set the global rules. In the words of the World Commission on the Social Dimensions of Globalization (WCSDG), a high-level multipartite group organized under the auspices of the International Labour Organization: "[T]he rules and institutions [of globalization] are unfair to poor countries, both in the ways they were drawn up and in their impact" (WCSDG 2004:52).

BOX 1 A Socially Just Globalization

Despite the critiques of contemporary globalization that characterize civil society mobilizations around the world, the bulk of this new social movement is not anti-globalization. If anything, as George Monbiot (2003) writes, we are insufficiently globalized, allowing international capital flows and trade in goods and services to slowly create a global marketplace, but with no effective forms of global citizen representa-

tion or governance. There is a need to critique the present form of globalization, as well as to articulate a clear vision of alternatives. Thus, the 2001 World Social Forum Charter of Principles states that it stands "in opposition to a process of globalisation commanded by the large multinational corporations and by the governments and international institutions at the service of those corporations' interests, with the complicity of national governments;" while it is committed to "alternatives...designed to ensure that globalisation in solidarity will prevail as a new stage in world history. This will respect universal human rights, and those of all citizens - men and women - of all nations and the environment and will rest on democratic international systems and institutions at the service of social justice, equality and the sovereignty of peoples" (World Social Forum Charter of Principles 2001). The World Commission on the Social Dimensions of Globalisation adopted a strikingly similar tone, arguing that today's globalization "has developed in an ethical vacuum" (2004:7), urging an "ethical globalization" based on human rights, gender equality, reduced disparity and environmental sustainability (p.5).

The causal pathways that link globalization with the illness or injury of particular individuals are often non-linear, involving multiple intervening variables and feedback loops (Woodward et al. 2001; Labonte & Torgerson 2003). Individual circumstances and opportunities are still shaped by the policy decisions of national and local governments. For example, HIV prevalence rates during the 1990s fell in Uganda, but rose in South Africa. Why? "It is difficult to link changes in HIV prevalence to specific policies or individual interventions, and any broad epidemiological and policy evaluation statements would clearly be simplifications" (Parkhurst & Lush 2004:1916). However, the authors of this statement go on to contrast Uganda's "early active governmental response," including willingness to support and work with civil society organizations, with South African political leaders' reluctance to place HIV prevention and treatment high on the national agenda. The result was to squander the advantage provided by a much better health infrastructure inherited from the apartheid-era government".[2] Patrick Bond (2001: 179-182), who directs the Centre for Civil Society at the University of KwaZulu-Natal, argues that South African reluctance to mobilize resources for treatment can be traced to the fact that AIDS "is killing workers and low-income consumers" – members of a population that is largely expendable for purposes of macroeconomic policy – "when South African elites in any case are adopting capital-intensive, export-oriented accumulation strategies." As another illustration of the importance of national policies, compare the effect of tax and transfer programs on child poverty, a crucial determinant of health, in Canada, the United States and Sweden – countries that define distinct points in the typology of welfare states (Esping-Anderson 1990) (Figure 1) – and the differences between these three countries on a number of health-relevant indicators (Figure 2).

Figure 1: Child Poverty Rates Before and After Taxes/Transfers

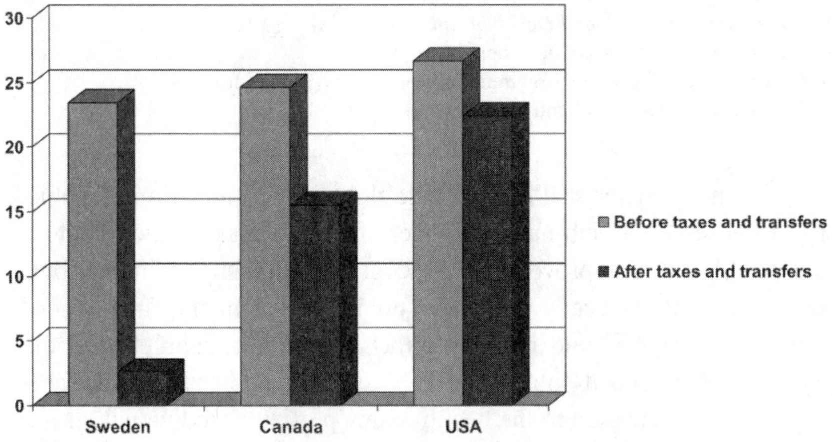

Source: Figure 9, *A League Table of Child Poverty in Rich Nations,* 2000. Innocenti Report Card #1, UNICEF. http://www.unicef-icdc.org/publications (data for most recent year before 2000 for which data available)

Figure 2: Selected Social Indicators, Sweden, Canada and the USA, 1995 - 2001

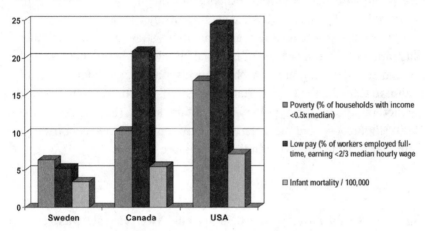

Sources: Jackson, A. 2002. *Canada Beats USA – But Loses Gold to Sweden: Twenty-Five Key Indicators of Social Development*
Canadian Council on Social Development,
http://www.ccsd.ca/pubs/2002/olympic/indicators.htm (figures for various years between 1995 and 2001)

National policies still matter. But globalization may limit the ability of national and sub-national governments to make policy choices that would lead to improvements in peoples' health, such as redistributing wealth, either directly or through public provision and financing of goods and services, and regulating the operation of markets and the activities of for-profit enterprises. The more steps in the causal pathway from globalization to the health of any particular individual, group or community, the more difficult it becomes to describe the web of causation – especially to audiences that may be skeptical because of their own privileged positions in the global order, or sympathetic but unaccustomed to arguments about causation that are not based on experimental situations where all but one variable can be carefully controlled. The real world does not work like that, and in order to address these difficulties we first draw some definitional boundaries around globalization and extract a few health lessons from its history.

BOX 2 The Erosion of Health

The last 150 years witnessed dramatic health improvements world-wide. Beginning in Europe and other wealthier countries in the late 19th through mid-20th centuries, better health quickly spread around the globe. The most dramatic gains over the past half-century occurred in poorer countries, substantially closing the 'health gap' that previously separated the northern industrialized and southern agrarian worlds. These health gains are attributed to increasing incomes, which improve diet and living conditions; improvements in public health measures, such as potable (safe) water and sanitation; and the diffusion of medical innovations, notably immunization and antibiotics (World Bank 1993).

Perhaps for the first time since the influenza pandemic of 1918-19, substantial reversals of this trend are evident for reasons other than war. These reversals affect the poorest and most vulnerable households, communities and nations, leading to widening gaps in health status that parallel disparities in income and wealth. First amongst the causes of these reversals is the pandemic of HIV/AIDS that, alongside other infectious diseases, disproportionately affect poorer populations in Africa, Asia and parts of Latin America. On average, a child born in Japan can expect to live 75 years; a child born in Malawi, Niger or Sierra Leone will not survive past 30 (Bloom & Canning 2003:48). Second, and almost equally disturbing, has been the collapse of the health and welfare infrastructure of the former Soviet Union: one and half million premature deaths between 1990 and 1995 are attributed to Russia's chaotic and often criminal transition to a market economy (Bloom & Canning 2003:59).

More than 10 million children under 5 years of age still die every year in low- and middle-income countries. Only 370,000 of those deaths are attributable to HIV/AIDS. Lower respiratory diseases, diarrhoeal disease and malaria – all of them predominantly diseases of poverty – account for 4.4 million of these deaths each year (WHO 2003:12). At the same time, many people in low- and middle-income countries now face a 'double burden' of disease, as rapid transition to patterns of production and consumption more typical of high-income nations increases their exposure to industrial pollution and to risk factors for cardiovascular disease, cancer and diabetes (Sen & Bonita 2000, Yach 2001, WHO 2003). Road accidents in low- and middle-income countries kill more than 1.1 million people each year, most of who never had the chance to own a vehicle (WHO 2003, Nantulya et al eds. 2003). Recent literature now refers to the triple or even quadruple burdens of disease, because of special challenges presented by rapid increases in injuries and by HIV/AIDS (Bradshaw et al 2003).

2 Globalization: From Trading Blankets to Global Warming

Globalization is best described as "a *process* of greater integration within the world economy through movements of goods and services, capital, technology and (to a lesser extent) labour, which lead increasingly to economic decisions being influenced by global conditions" (Jenkins 2004:1). The focus of this book is on trade liberalization (increasing the cross-border flow of goods) and deregulation of national and international financial markets (facilitating rapid transnational movements of capital). Historically, the transnational movement of people has been a crucial element of globalization, and to some extent it remains so today. Over 175 million people lived outside their country of birth in 2000. Remittances of foreign-born workers to their low- or middle-income countries of origin – some $80 billion in 2002, more than double the amount in 1990 – have become an important source of foreign currency for many countries (Kapur & McHale 2003). Nevertheless, large-scale migration remains "the missing flow in today's globalisation" (Dollar 2002:33), mainly because of "policy changes in one dominant nation, the United States, which has switched from a protectionist welcoming immigrants to a free trader restricting their entrance" (Williamson 2002:7).

BOX 3 Global Political Economy Terms

Discussions of global political economy feature a number of specialized terms that may be unfamiliar to general readers. These include:

Balance of payments *The difference between the amount of foreign currency coming into a country from sales of exports and the amount leaving to pay for imports; plus net receipts (or minus net payments) of interest, profits on foreign investment, etc; plus net inflows (or minus net outflows) of funds in the form of aid, loans, foreign investment, etc.*

Free trade *Reduction of tariff and non-tariff barriers to the cross-border flow of goods and services. A tariff is simply a tax on the value of* *imports of goods or services, levied at the border. Non-tariff barriers are policies that act as barriers to imports without imposing a tariff - for instance, requirements that all imports of a particular kind of good meet the importing country's regulatory standards, or be labelled in a certain way.*

GDP/GNP/GNI *Gross domestic product (GDP) is the total value of all final goods and services produced in a country in a year. Gross national product (GNP) is GDP plus property income and employee compensation from abroad. Gross national income (GNI) is for practical purposes the same as GNP.*

Neoliberalism *A political and economic ideology that emphasizes free markets over state regulation, repudiates redistributive policies such as progressive taxation (see below), favours private over public sector provision of goods and services, and attaches especially high priority to maintaining low inflation rates. One consequence of this obsession with low inflation is that creditors benefit, while debtors lose. Neoliberalism was and is exemplified by the domestic economic policies adopted by the Thatcher government in the UK, and (with some crucial variations, primarily involving the use of government deficits to finance military spending and tax cuts) by the Reagan and George W Bush governments in the US.*

Progressive/regressive taxes *A progressive tax is one that falls proportionately more heavily on higher income people or households, relative to their incomes. This includes income tax in which the marginal rate (the tax rate charged on each additional dollar of income) goes up as the taxpayer's income increases. A regressive tax is one that falls more heavily on lower-income people or households, relative to their incomes. Most sales and consumption taxes are regressive (because low-income households must spend proportionately more of what they earn).*

Washington consensus *A term coined by Williamson (1990) to capture the key reforms that the US government tried to promote for developing countries in the 1980s, including free trade (in particular, lowering barriers to imports) and financial market liberalization, privatization, and currency devaluation.*

Globalization is not new. The history of humankind has been one of pushing against borders, exploring, expanding, trading, conquering and assimilating (Diamond 1997). By the 16th century the geographic and resource endowments of Europe, combined with new sailing and navigation technologies, ushered in the first truly global era of colonization and trade. Some argue that exploitation of colonial wealth was an important factor in the rise and eventual global dominance of Western capitalism, while ensuring the continued poverty of many former colonies (Galeano 1973). A more nuanced account says colonial trade was fuelled primarily by the surging income of a small number of European landowners and their demand for global exotica (Williamson 2002), suggesting that rising income inequalities, which characterized 15th and 16th century Europe, can represent both a driving force and a consequence of increased global trade. Williamson credits the end of the Napoleonic wars and a "global *pax Britannica*" in 1820 with the start of a world regime of globalization in which "the liberal dismantling of mercantilism" and "declining transport costs...worked together to produce truly global commodity markets across the nineteenth century."

Globalization came to a temporary halt in the early 20th century with two world wars and the Great Depression. The ensuing devastation spurred the creation of new international organizations to promote reconstruction and development, in an effort to avoid the economic shocks that partly underpinned both wars (WCSDG 2004). The United Nations would provide political oversight to global peace and development. The International Monetary Fund (IMF) would maintain global economic stability by helping countries with balance of payments problems[3] (see Box 3). The World Bank would provide concessional (low interest) loans or grants for post-war reconstruction and, later, for global development. The General Agreement on Tariffs and Trade (GATT) would be a venue for negotiating the removal of protectionist barriers to international trade. Globalization was back on track (Williamson 2002:7), even if its new rules and institutions represented the interests of the world's dominant, victorious nations, and even if international trade as a percentage of global economic output did not reach levels characteristic of the late 19th and early 20th centuries until the 1990s (Cameron & Stein 2000). The collapse of the USSR and the fall of the

Berlin Wall, marking the end of an ideological counterweight to an already ascendant neo-liberal form of capitalism, arguably accelerated the pace of global market integration and certainly enhanced its legitimacy.

International trade in goods is only one dimension of globalization. Several other trends reveal how and why today's globalization differs from earlier eras:

The scale of international private financial flows resulting from capital market liberalization. Aided by technologies that allow '24/7' global trade and new forms of finance capital such as hedge funds and derivatives, currency transactions worth between $1.5 and 2 trillion occur daily.[4] Much of this activity involves speculative portfolio money chasing short-term changes in currency valuations, rather than foreign direct investment (FDI) that may go into new growth-promoting productive capacity. (We emphasize *may* since much FDI, particularly in Latin America, has gone into buying privatized state assets, representing a change in ownership rather than new growth-promoting production; see Corner House 2001, UNCTAD 2004a).[5] The scale of these transactions dwarfs the total foreign exchange reserves of all governments, reducing their ability to intervene in foreign exchange markets to stabilize their currencies, manage their economies and maintain fiscal autonomy (UNDP 1999). Each country experiencing a 'currency crisis' has seen increased poverty and inequality, and decreased health and social spending (O'Brien 2002; Cobham, 2002); with women and children disproportionately bearing the burden (Gyebi et al. 2002).

BOX 4 From Casino Capitalism to Climate Change

International relations scholar Susan Strange (1986) coined the term "casino capitalism" to describe the volatile flow of speculative finance surging through world capital markets. As "hot money" enters a country, usually after it first opens its capital accounts to outside investors, its exchange into the local currency increases the currency's value on the "forex" (foreign exchange) market. After a period of currency inflation, the more aggressive casino capitalists begin to move their investments elsewhere, precipitating a rapid plunge in the currency's exchange value as speculators' herd behaviour kicks in (WCSDG 2004) and the hot money leaves as rapidly as it entered.

One such crisis was the Brazilian currency meltdown of 1998, a result of the greatest inflow and outflow of speculative capital ever experienced by a developing country (de Paula and Alves Jr 2000). The Brazilian government lacked sufficient foreign reserves to stabilize its currency and was forced to borrow from the IMF, whose rescue package came with several conditionalities, including the requirement for drastic public spending cuts. These cuts extended to Brazil's environmental protection spending, which was slashed by two thirds, leading to the collapse of a multinational project (Brazil could no longer pay its agreed upon portion of the cost) that would have begun satellite mapping of the Amazonian rainforest as a first step in stemming its destruction. This destruction, in turn, will almost certainly have a profound effect on climate change, because of the rainforest's role in sequestering carbon dioxide, with long-term and potentially severe health implications for much of the world's population (Labonte 1999).

The establishment of binding rules, primarily through the World Trade Organization, the successor to the GATT. WTO and other regional or bilateral trade agreements have established enforceable supra-national obligations on states, and have expanded to include services, investment and government purchases. Countries have also entered into multilateral covenants and treaties on human rights and environmental protection. Notably, the 1948 Universal Declaration on Human Rights[6] purportedly protects individuals and groups against state repression or discrimination, while obliging states to take "progressive measures, national and international, to secure ... universal and effective recognition and observance" of a package of rights including "a standard of living adequate for the health and well-being of [oneself] and of his family, including food, clothing, housing and medical care and necessary social services, and the right to security in the event of unemployment, sickness, disability, widowhood, old age or other lack of livelihood in circumstances beyond his control" (Article 25). These desiderata were expanded upon in the 1966 International Covenants on Civil and Political Rights and on Economic, Social and Cultural Rights. Even though the latter are treaties and therefore binding on signatory countries that have ratified them (in the case of Economic, Social and Cultural Rights, conspicuously not including the United States) as a matter of international law, they are unlike trade agreements in that no economic interests drive their enforcement through the limited mechanisms that are available. This asymmetry between enforceable economic (market-based) rules and social and environmental obligations may represent the biggest governance challenge of the new millennium, an "imbalance between the economy and the polity [that] is undermining democratic accountability" (WCSDG 2004:4). Market-based rules are themselves asymmetrical, since their primary enforcement measures – trade sanctions – can be used effectively by a large and wealthy economy, but invariably hurt a small and poorer economy (Jawara & Kwa 2003).[7]

Reorganization of production across national borders. This third trend is one of the most significant characteristics of our contemporary global political economy (Dicken 2003). Multinational enterprises (MNEs), several of which are economically larger than many nations or whole regions, are central to this process. In 2000, 51 of the world's largest 100 economic entities were corporations (Anderson & Cavanagh 2000); 49 were nation-states. At least one third of global trade is intra-firm trade between affiliated companies (WCSDG 2004:32), in which an MNE's subsidiary in one country sells parts or products to a subsidiary in another country (Reinicke 1998). Even this figure understates the global integration of production, because it does not reflect production or commodity chains that involve a core firm in flexible, often short-term contractual relationships with multiple suppliers (Milberg 2004). The emergence of such global production or commodity chains (Donaghu & Barff 1990, Gereffi & Korzeniewicz eds. 1994, Gereffi 1999) allows MNEs to locate labour intensive operations in low-wage countries (often in exclusive export processing zones or EPZs), carry out research and development in countries with high levels of publicly funded education and public investment in research, and declare most of their profits in low-tax countries. The result is global tax competition and lower corporate tax revenues in all countries (Grunberg 1998, Wade 2003).

These changes did not 'just happen.' They required policy decisions by governments around the world (Marchak 1991, Gershman &

Irwin 2000), decisions from which most affected citizens were often excluded. During the 1990s, the breadth and depth of that exclusion generated a global social movement that was, if not actively hostile to globalization, at least profoundly skeptical about the claims made by its cheerleaders. This movement received considerable media attention as a result of protests during meetings of the WTO, the G8,[8] the World Bank and IMF and the World Economic Forum. However, its social justice and environmental sustainability concerns have long shaped grass-roots campaigns in low- and middle-income countries, and the quality of its research and advocacy have compelled grudging acceptance of such campaigns' legitimacy even on the part of those who profoundly disagree with their conclusions.

Health concerns have been slower to enter the globalization debate than environmental, social or economic issues (Deaton 2004b), although the relation between health and globalization is far from new. Disease and pestilence have long followed trade routes from one part of the world to another. Rats on trading ships spread plague, resulting in the deaths of an estimated one-quarter of Western Europe's population in the 14th century. British trade, buttressed by imperialism, helped transform cholera from a problem in a few rural areas of India into a 19th century pandemic (Ringen 1979). Blankets infected with small-pox played no small role in decimating the indigenous populations of North America – just one of many instances in which European diseases killed off colonized peoples (Diamond 1997:210-212). Trade-related diseases also strained relationships between the captains of industry and the stewards of public health (Ringen 1979), with merchants frequently resisting quarantines on goods as unnecessarily trade-restrictive, although not above using quarantines to restrict competitive trade that might hurt their interests (Deaton 2004b). Some of these patterns persist today. A Chinese merchant ship was the source of Latin America's cholera outbreak in 1991, which resulted in 10,000 deaths (Kickbusch & Buse 2001). An influx of Asian longhorn beetles, hiding in wooden shipping crates, threatens North American forests. Increased marketing of tobacco products by MNEs and the 'export' (through local production and global branding) of diets high in sugar or fat contribute to rising rates of chronic disease in low-income countries (Lee 2001, Mackay & Ericksen 2002, Lang 2003, Weatherspoon & Reardon 2003).

The economic costs associated with the 2003 outbreak of Severe Acute Respiratory Syndrome (SARS) alerted many high-income countries to the value of global infection control. But the increased spread of communicable diseases or unhealthy consumption by trade vector is only a small part of the globalization/health relationship. Of far more importance is how globalization affects such health determinants as poverty and inequality, and here we confront the dominant story of globalization's health benefits.

3 Globalization's 'Poster Children'

China, India and a handful of East Asian countries are often used to support the so-called 'rising tide' story about globalization in which sustained economic growth leads to higher standards of living and better health for all – a rising tide that lifts all boats. China, in particular, is increasingly cited as a model for what global market integration can do for a developing country, because it has experienced phenomenal economic growth since introducing selective internal economic reforms and beginning aggressively to pursue export markets and foreign direct investment.[9] Understanding the source of that growth, and the reason China may rival the United States as the world's largest economy within the next two decades (Ramo 2004), is as easy as looking at the labels on merchandise at the local Wal-Mart, a US-based retailer that is now the world's largest corporation, ranked by sales, and the largest employer in both the USA and Mexico. Wal-Mart has consolidated its dominance of the mass-market retail sector by relentlessly squeezing suppliers – many of them in China – to reduce costs, which may also have inhibited progress toward higher labour standards (Kaufman 2000, Goodman & Pan 2004). India's growth during the 1980s and 1990s, though not as spectacular — about 4 percent annual growth in GDP/per capita over the 1990s (Dollar 2002) — was nonetheless impressive. That 38 percent of the world's people live in India and China also gives those countries special status in the 'rising tide' globalization story that is familiar in the pages of *The Economist* and *The Financial Times*, the speeches of European and North American trade ministers and the work of many (but not all) World Bank economists.

The story starts from the premise that increased trade and foreign investment improve economic growth, which increases wealth and reduces poverty, leading to improved health. In addition, increased wealth can sustain investment in public provision of such services as health care, education and water/sanitation. Improved education and population health both accelerate economic growth, and so the circle virtuously closes upon itself. This set of claims is important because it underscores the positive contribution of improved population health to economic growth. Notably, the World Health Organization's Commission on Macroeconomics and Health (2001) has shown that improved health is not simply a product of economic growth, but also foundational to it. Nobel Prize-winning economist Amartya Sen (2000) attributes China's more rapid growth, as compared to India's, to its pre-market emphasis on public education and health care, which created a healthy, literate (but also cheap) labour force that became a source of comparative advantage.

At the same time, much is left out of the story.

Consider, first, the impact of globalization on poverty. This is of fundamental public health importance since poverty is one of the most powerful predictors of poor health for individuals or nations[10]. It is claimed that globalization-driven growth has reduced the number of people living in abject poverty worldwide (defined by the World Bank as living on less than $1/day) by 200 million since 1980 (Dollar 2002). According to the most recent estimates this still leaves 1.2 billion people around the world living on less than $1/day, and 2.8 billion, almost half the world's population, on less than $2/day (Chen & Ravallion 2004). As Wade (2002:50) comments acerbically, "all the thunder and lightning about trends can divert attention from what should be our central preoccupation, the sheer magnitude of poverty and inequality." Apart from this ethical issue, critics point to flaws in how the Bank measures poverty (Wade 2002, 2004, Reddy & Pogge 2003), questionable use of historical data (Wade 2004), the irrelevance of the $1 a day threshold to the realities of life in the developing world's fast-growing cities (Satterthwaite 2003), and lack of reliable data from China and India where almost all of the poverty reduction has taken place (Wade 2002). In India, new research finds that poverty probably increased during the 1990s, as did rural hunger (Patnaik 2004).

Even if we concede that recent growth in China and India has reduced the number of their people living in extreme poverty, although we can't be certain of the number (Wade 2002, Deaton 2004a), poverty increased in many regions over this same period. They include sub-Saharan Africa (SSA), Eastern Europe, Central Asia and, until the early 1990s, Latin America. On either the $1/day or $2/day measure, the number of people living in poverty in SSA roughly doubled between 1981 and 2001 (Chen & Ravallion 2004:Table 4). Modest economic growth in Latin America from 1990 – 1997 cut poverty rates by 5 per cent, but the Asian-precipitated recession in the late 1990s caused poverty to rise again, with almost 44 per cent of the Latin American population living below official poverty lines in 2002 (UN Habitat 2003a).

Why? Enthusiasts of globalization argue that countries that open themselves to the global economy grow, while those that retain outdated forms of protectionism languish (Dollar 2001, Dollar & Kraay 2000). But reality is more complicated, in at least two respects.

First, those countries held up as model high-performing globalizers (China, India, Malaysia, Thailand and Vietnam) actually started out as more closed economies than the countries whose economies stalled or declined, mostly in Africa and Latin America (Dollar 2002). The sleight-of-hand lies in definition. Dollar's (2002) 'globalizers' are countries that saw their trade/GDP ratio increase since 1977; his 'non-globalizers' are simply those that saw their ratio drop. But his non-globalizers were already twice as integrated into the world economy in 1977, a degree of integration his supposed globalizers did not reach until the late 1990s. There is, in fact, a long and contentious debate amongst development economists over the impacts of liberalization on growth and poverty reduction, much of it directly challenging Dollar's and Dollar & Kraay's conclusions on theoretical, methodological and empirical grounds (e.g. Rodrik 1999, 2001, Rodriguez & Rodrik 2000). It can be argued that the problem for the non-performers was not their retreat from globalization, but their high dependency on natural resources and primary commodities (Milanovic 2003).

Second, the performing globalizers, notably China and India, experienced much of their poverty-reducing growth *before* they began to reduce their import tariffs and open themselves to foreign investment (Wade 2002). Like Japan, South Korea and Taiwan before them, China and India grew behind walls of import protection for their domestic producers, strict controls over banking and investment, and (at least in the case of China) direct and indirect subsidies for exporters. They liberalized trade only as they became richer. Economic historian Ha-Joon Chang (2002) shows that this was precisely how European and North

American countries grew their wealth a century earlier, and that to deny low- and middle-income countries the opportunity to do the same today through new trade rules amounts to "kicking away the ladder".

BOX 5 Winners, Losers and Immiserizing Growth

Defenders of global market integration often claim that low- and middle-income countries, excluding Africa, have benefited most. This is a misleading or at best overstated claim. A recent scorecard provides evidence that globalization has been far from equal in distributing its benefits (Weisbrot et al. 2001). It compares health, economic and development indicators for the pre-globalization (1960-1980) and rapidly globalizing (1980-2000) periods. During the globalizing period, economic growth per capita declined in all countries, but declined most rapidly for the poorest 20% of nations. The rate of improvement in life expectancy declined for all but the wealthiest 20% of nations, indicating increasing global disparity. Infant and child mortality improvements slowed, particularly for the poorest 40%. The rate of growth of public spending on education also slowed for all countries, and the rate of growth for school enrolment, literacy rates and other educational attainment measures slowed for most of the poorest 40%.

In a similar study former World Bank economist Branko Milanovic compared population-adjusted annual growth rates for different regions of the world for 1960-1978 and 1978-1998. After Asia, the high-income countries of western Europe, North America and Oceania (meaning Australia and Aotearoa/New Zealand) came out ahead of the rest of the global pack. "Maintaining that globalization as we know it is the way to go and that, if the Washington consensus policies have not borne fruit so far, they will surely do so, is to replace empiricism with ideology," he concludes (Milanovic 2003).

Evidence on this point is provided by a recent study concluding that economic growth through global market integration for South Africa, a middle-income country with a strong private sector and relatively skilled cheap labour, can only be maintained through "sustained currency depreciation." The larger the share of traded goods in GDP (an increasing ratio as globalization proceeds), the more likely is an outcome of "immiserizing growth", as the international purchasing power of domestic income growth is eroded (Kaplinsky, Morris & Redman 2002).

Two key elements of the mainstream story, then – that liberalization reduces poverty and promotes growth – are shaky at best, and wrong as global generalizations. What, then, of the third, that globalization is having no health-damaging effect on income inequalities? Whether, or how, income inequalities that do not involve absolute poverty affect population health remains a disputed point amongst health researchers (Deaton 2001)[11]. Poverty, which is higher in high income-inequality countries, may be the bigger problem whether it is defined in absolute or relative terms. But greater inequality of income or wealth makes it harder for economic growth to lift people out of poverty. Moreover, income inequalities continue to be associated with declines in social cohesion, public support for state redistributive social policies (Deaton 2001, Global Social Policy Forum 2001, Gough 2001), and even political engagement (Solt 2004); as well as with higher rates of infant mortality, homicide, and suicide, and generalized conflict (Deaton 2001). Cross-national studies find that income inequalities can actually dampen longer-term economic growth (Easterly 2002), delaying the health gains such growth might bring or sustain. Finally, rising income inequalities, particularly between nations, may increase corruption (as elites in poorer countries try to match the wealth of those in richer ones), the global 'brain drain' (as educated persons migrate from poorer to richer nations), and ever more desperate attempts by the remaining "vagabonds" to seek illegal entry (Wade 2002) – a point dramatically illustrated by the militarization and fortification of the US-Mexican border. Income inequalities *do* matter.

But are they rising? The conflicting answers here depend on what measures are used and what units are measured (Dollar 2002, Wade 2002, Deaton 2004a). Income inequalities *within* many countries are rising. On some measures, income inequalities *between* countries are also increasing (Milanovic 2003). Poverty reduction in China and India, with their large populations, means that income inequalities between individuals across the world may be declining slightly, although there is disagreement even here. The more important question is globalization's impact on these trends. Some economists claim that, because there is no consistent relationship between globalization and within-country inequalities, we shouldn't worry; on average, the 'rising tide' lifts all boats more or less equally (Dollar & Kraay 2000, Dollar

2002)[12]. But simple arithmetic tells a different story. Consider two people, one earning the equivalent of $50,000/year and another earning $500/year — a not atypical situation in countries like India or China. If each person's income rises by 10 per cent, the effect is to increase *absolute* inequality between these two persons by an astounding $4,950. To the extent that one's income or wealth corresponds to political influence and power, these absolute differences should concern us.

This returns us to the story of the Chinese student who killed himself, and how it relates to the broader trends sketched above. The key link is China's domestic market reforms, which while credited with rapid growth have also drastically increased economic inequalities. The Gini coefficient in China, a standard measure of income inequality, was a low 28.8 in 1981 but reached 41.5 in 1995, a level similar to the USA (Chen & Wang 2001). The rural-urban divide is increasing, regional disparities are widening and access to opportunities is becoming less equal: during the 1990s, only the incomes of the richest quintile of the population grew faster than the national average – again, a trend remarkably similar to the US (Chen & Wang 2001). Similar trends exist in India, Vietnam, Brazil and other countries experiencing rapid liberalization, rapid growth or both.[13] And in all these countries, inequalities may be rising even within 'rich' regions, as they are within many industrialized countries (Cornia, Addison & Kiiski 2004).

Many health indicators at the population level, such as infant and under-5 mortality, in those countries where inequalities increased (China, Vietnam and India) actually improved over the past decade; however, immunization rates for one-year-old children saw "significant regression" in all three countries (Social Watch 2004:70-75). But aggregate data hide important changes in intra-national, interregional and other inter-group inequalities. Thus, gender-related health inequalities in China increased; a longitudinal survey in several Chinese provinces found that the percentage of women with insurance coverage for prenatal and delivery services fell from 58.3 percent in 1989 to 34.7 percent in 1997 (Akin, Dow Lance 2004:300). Health disparities between rural regions and the cities also increased (Liu et al. 2001). This is no doubt partly because China's market reforms not only increased economic inequality, but also led to the collapse of its once vanguard systems of employment- and community-based health insurance.

The government share of health expenditures fell by over half between 1980 and 1998, almost trebling the portion paid by families (Liu, Rao & Hsiao 2003). This led to the growth of private delivery systems for those who could afford them, and increased cost-recovery schemes for services that were still under some form of public health insurance. The result was two-fold. There was a surge in the number of people who fell into poverty by exhausting their income and savings to pay for medical treatment – Qingming's grandfather was just one of 27 million rural Chinese in 1998 to whom this happened (Liu, Rao & Hsiao 2003). There was also a dramatic slowdown in China's population health improvements (Deaton 2004b), particularly infant mortality and life expectancy (Akin, Dow & Lance 2004). The longitudinal survey cited above found that insurance coverage, already available to just one in four Chinese in 1989, continued to decline slowly through the 1990s, with a rapid decline in coverage in cities, but an increase in rural areas (from 7.4% to 14.5%) as a result of a number of pilot schemes aimed at recreating some form of the insurance once provided through agricultural collectives (Akin, Dow & Lance 2004).

Similar trends are found in India, where rural poverty has deepened in many states and is associated with marked health disparities. Women in the poorer Indian states are particularly disadvantaged, experiencing shorter life expectancies and lower literacy rates than men (Abbasi 1999:1133). Government expenditure on health care accounted for just 17.9 percent of India's health care spending, with the remainder financed out of users' pockets – making India's health care system one of the world's most highly privatized (World Health Organization 2004:138-139). Predictably, quality of public health services is low and deteriorating; the infant mortality rate for the poorest 20 percent of the population is 2.5 times higher than for the richest 20 percent; and a child in the "Low standard of living" group is almost four times as likely to die in childhood as a child in the "High standard of living" group (International Institute for Population Sciences & ORC Macro 2004).

What if Qingming had completed his education and found employment in one the many export processing zones (EPZs) to which an estimated 10 to 20 million rural Chinese migrate each year (AFL-CIO 2004:14)? EPZs have proliferated throughout the developing world in the past two decades, with "the free trade, foreign investment and export-driven ethos of the modern economy…transform[ing] them into 'vehicles of globalization'" (ILO 1998).[14] Between 40 million (ILO 2004a) and 50 million (Howard 2004) workers were employed in some 5,000 EPZs in 2004, 75 per cent of them in China alone (ILO 2004a). Migration from rural to urban areas and the expansion of megacities create a new set of health crises. Rarely, if ever, are public resources sufficient to provide the housing, water, sanitation or energy infrastructure essential to managing this growth. Indeed, the most recent report of the United Nations Human Settlements Programme makes the point that the elements of globalization we describe (the market reforms of liberalization, privatization and de-regulation) are largely to blame for the worldwide growth of slums and the lack of public resources to cope with them (UN Habitat 2003b). This Report also makes the important point that the rising wealth of globalization's *nouveau riche* winners creates inflationary pressure on most goods and services, but particularly on land and housing – which only worsens conditions for globalization's losers. To understand this point, North American readers need only consider what has happened to housing prices in their own fast-growing cities, especially when rent controls have been eased or lifted.

Qingming would also have been exposed to the hazardous working conditions associated with most EPZs. While some countries extend national labour laws and protections to their EPZs, exceptions, violations and union-free policies are commonplace (ILO 1998). Hours are frequently long, the work is generally repetitive and arduous, and even minimal social 'safety nets' are lacking. This leads to pervasive stress and fatigue (ILO 1998), and practices such as locking in workers have led to numerous deaths and injuries when fires have broken out in factories (ICFTU 2003). Hours of work and wages in China's EPZs are effectively unregulated; many people work 12-18-hour days, seven days a week, for months at a time. "Death by overworking" – or *guolaosi* – has become a commonly used term in contemporary China, and it is not used metaphorically. Workplace accidents reportedly killed 140,000 workers in China in 2003, an annual death toll of one in every 250 Chinese workers (AFL-CIO 2004).

China led the world in the amount of foreign investment it received in 2002, and was second only to the USA in 2003 (China Daily 2004).

Investors do not act from altruism: it is simply more profitable to produce goods in the world's largest supplier of cheap, healthy, compliant and non-unionized labour than it is almost anywhere else. Labour critics, such as the AFL-CIO in the USA (2004) and the Independent Confederation of Free Trade Unions, argue that China's "blatant disregard for workers' rights" (ICFTU 2003:5) is leading firms to relocate production to China from EPZs elsewhere in the world with somewhat less destructive working conditions. Employment in Mexico's *maquiladoras*, that country's EPZs, dropped from 1.3 million in 2000 to 1 million in 2002 as production shifted to China, where "inflation-adjusted manufacturing wages have fallen in the last decade, while labour productivity has rapidly increased from year-to-year" (AFL-CIO 2004:15).

BOX 6   Gendered Face of EPZs

Had Qingming found work in an export processing zone (EPZ), his sex would have placed him in the minority. EPZ employers favour young, often single women, particularly in textile, garment manufacturing and electronics assembly: their fingers are thought to be more nimble than men's, and they are often cheaper, receiving only 50-80% of the wages paid to men (ICFTU 2003). Eighty per cent of China's EPZ employees are women (Durano 2002); the global average is 70-90% (Athreya 2003). EPZ employment for women is credited with increasing gender empowerment by providing them with income. This may sometimes be true, but women's earnings are often channelled back to the control of male family members, and many women's domestic responsibilities remain unchanged, creating a double burden of work (Durano 2002). To reduce costs, EPZs frequently employ women on part-time, casual or subcontracting arrangements that involve working at home. This gives women flexibility between their domestic and paid duties, but denies them the social protections that might come with regular forms of employment (Durano 2002).

EPZs, because they are located in countries with a large supply of cheap labour, rarely improve wage conditions for either women or men (ICFTU 2003). Workers are plentiful so there is little incentive for enterprises to train and retain their staff. Technology transfer, one of the key means by which low- and middle-income countries can improve their domestic economic efficiency and performance, is rare. Liberalization of financial markets means that little of the foreign currency that enters the EPZs stays in the host country. To attract foreign investment in EPZs, countries often offer extensive tax holidays (ILO 1998). By definition, these zones do not levy tariffs on imported materials, further limiting the tax benefits a country might receive for redistribution as health, education and other development investments. In many instances few locally produced goods are used in the EPZs. In 30 years of maquiladoras (as EPZs are called in Mexico), only 2% of the raw goods processed came from within the country (ILO 1998). Apart from the jobs created, some of which are now departing to China, the EPZs have had little positive impact on Mexico's overall economic development. They may help countries develop their internal economies, but only if there are strong "backward and forward linkages" - requirements that companies in EPZs purchase raw materials from, and transfer new technologies to, the host country through partnerships with local firms outside the special zones (Wade 2002).

Perhaps, with time, greater equality, employment security and safe working conditions – all essential to sustained population health – will return to China, and to other rapidly liberalizing countries. A recent essay that makes this claim also highlights concerns about rapidly rising inequalities, leaving open the question of how equitably the benefits of future growth will be shared, and of the implications for population health and health equity (Ramo 2004). Answering such questions as they relate to any specific country or region must be left to country and area specialists. However, even if the conclusion is that growth will, eventually, lead to widely shared improvements in health –as it did in England during the second half of the 19th century (Szreter 1999) – an important ethical question remains. How long may those whose health is negatively affected by globalization, or more probably their survivors, legitimately be asked to wait for such improvements?

4 AIDS, Poverty, and the Poverty of Aid

Our second vignette raises the question of the rich world's responsibilities for ensuring healthier globalization. It also shows that much more is required of a global political economy than simply more, faster and fairer growth if health equity is to be an outcome.

As noted earlier, causal pathways that link globalization with the illness of particular individuals are often not linear or straightforward. However, it is plausible to link Chileshe's HIV infection to the triumph of free markets, actively promoted by international agencies dominated by high-income countries. In 1992, as part of a structural adjustment program that was one of the conditions attached to loans from the International Monetary Fund, Zambia opened its borders to imports including cheap, second-hand clothing. Its domestic, state-run clothing manufacturers, admittedly inefficient in both technology and management by wealthier nation standards, produced more expensive and lower quality goods. They could not compete, especially when the importers had the advantage of no production costs and no import duties.[15] Within eight years, 132 of 140 clothing and textile mills closed operations and 30,000 jobs disappeared, which the World Bank acknowledges as "unintended and regrettable consequences" of the adjustment process (Jeter 2002). Many of the second-hand clothes that flooded Zambia and other SSA countries, ironically, began as donations to charities in Europe, the USA and Canada. Surpluses not needed for their own poor were sold to wholesalers, who exported them in bulk to Africa, earning up to 300 per cent or more on their costs (Jeter 2002). The scale of this exchange is not insignificant. Sales to SSA countries form the USA are worth about $60 million annually (Jeter 2002); in 2001, Canadian exports of *salaula* ("rummaging through the pile"), as used clothing is called in Zambia, valued over $25 million (Industry Canada 2002).

BOX 7 What is Structural Adjustment?

The World Bank initiated structural adjustment loans in 1980 to help developing countries respond to the impact of the 1979-1980 recession on their ability to service external debt. The Mexican debt crisis of 1982, the first of many around the world, saw the IMF and World Bank change into "watchdogs for developing countries, to keep them on a policy track that would help them repay most of their debts and to open their markets for international investors" (Junne 2001:206). The mechanism of this transformation was the provision of new loans to help with debt rescheduling, provided countries agreed to a relatively standard package of macroeconomic policies that included the following:

- *reduced subsidies for basic items of consumption;*

- *removal of barriers to imports and foreign direct investment;*

- *reductions in state expenditures, particularly on social programmes such as health, education, water/sanitation and housing, with recommended (not required) but usually ineffective targeting of special supports to the poor; and*

- *rapid privatization of state-owned enterprises, on the presumption that private service provision was inherently more efficient, and that proceeds from privatization could be used to ensure debt repayment (Milward 2000).*

It is sometimes argued that when structural adjustment failed it was because countries failed to implement it fully, and that their national economies were in such a mess when adjustment was imposed that their deterioration might have been worse without it. Many economists and historians disagree, and many African countries that had previously been buoyant began to slide into economic stagnation after adopting structural adjustment (UN Habitat 2003b). The recently established IMF Independent Evaluation Office found that over half the countries undertaking structural adjustment underperformed relative to theoretical expectations; that the assumed private sector recovery rarely occurred, or did so much more slowly than anticipated; and that the IMF's emphasis on taxing consumption, rather than income, fuelled domestic inequalities (IMF 2004). A recent UN report summarizes what can be guaranteed from a structural adjustment programme (UN Habitat 2003b):

- *The economy opens up and exports increase (in amount, but not necessarily in dollar value).*

- *The money supply normally undergoes a severe tightening and interest rates soar, so that investment stops and many smaller enterprises are unable to continue.*

- *The informal economy grows substantially due to the swelling unemployed and the removal of controls.*

- *Enterprises have a large burden of debt and the financial sector becomes technically insolvent.*

- *The urban poor bear a disproportionate share of the damage.*

- *Social safety nets are directed to politically powerful groups who may be disadvantaged, not to the poor.*

- *As with all neoliberal programmes, social insecurity in all its forms increases.*

The neoliberal assumptions of structural adjustment also embody multiple gender-related biases. A "deflationary bias" occurs when governments adopt policies that prioritize the interests of creditors and owners of capital. A "male breadwinner" bias "constructs the ownership of rights to make claims on the state for social benefits (access to services, cash transfers) around a norm of full-time, life-long working-age participation in the market-based labor force." A "commodification bias" occurs as public social provision (e.g. of education, health care, and care for children and the elderly) is replaced by market-based provision, with access differentiated by purchasing power (Elson and Cagatay 2000).

Political accountability is a fundamental issue. In almost every case, structural adjustment proved massively unpopular with citizens (Walton & Seddon 1994) as it became evident that it benefited elites over the poor, whose ranks were swelling with the downward mobility of the former middle class - and was often met with protests that were frequently, sometimes brutally suppressed.

For conventional economists, this is a textbook example of how and why trade liberalization works: Consumers get better and cheaper goods, in some cases goods they could not have afforded otherwise, and inefficient producers are driven out of business. However Chileshe's husband, and then Chileshe herself, paid a heavy price. It was a price that cascaded throughout other sectors of Zambia's limited manufacturing base, with some 40 per cent of manufacturing jobs disappearing during the 1990s (Jeter 2002). Manufacturing value added, as a per cent of GDP, fell by half over the 1990s; the comparable figure for industry value added was more than two-thirds (UN Habitat 2003b:Table B.6). A study of the impact of the IMF's adjustment reforms on manufacturing in five countries in sub-Saharan Africa, including Zambia, found only negative effects on firms' performances on a variety of measures, except for one: foreign businesses gained a slight advantage (Okoroafo 1997). A more detailed study of forty-three Zambian companies affirmed these findings and provided another: most MNEs "freely admitted...to using transfer pricing practices to channel income remission [offshore] by overpricing imports from abroad and/or under-pricing exports" (Muuka 1997), reducing the ability of Zambia to tax company profits. This is a common business practice, and indeed one of the significant advantages of operating on a multinational scale (Murray ed. 1981).

Large numbers of previously employed Zambian workers came to rely on the informal, ill-paid and untaxed underground economy. The privatization of state enterprises, another component of Zambia's adjustment program, eliminated a further source of revenues that might have been used to support social programs such as education and health care. (This problem was also encountered in many Latin American countries when structural adjustment led to the privatization of profitable, though admittedly inefficient, state telecommunications monopolies.) Other causes for the public revenue decline included a continuous slide in world prices for copper, Zambia's primary export commodity; Japan's 1990s recession (it was Zambia's main importer of copper); high debt service costs; declining levels of development assistance; and capital flight (WTO 1996, Lindsey 2002) – a problem discussed in greater detail in the next section of this book. Faced with precipitous public revenue declines and a lender preoccupation with 'cost recovery' in basic services, Zambia began in the 1990s to impose user charges for schools and health services. Not surprisingly, this was followed by a rapid rise in Zambia's school dropout and illiteracy rates, which are projected to double by 2015 (UN Habitat 2003b:Table B7), and costs became the main reason people failed to seek health care, or did not follow through on medical treatment (Atkinson et al. 1999).

The Zambian government is now seeking to undo many of these policies, eliminating user fees for education, reducing charges for public health care, and reintroducing agricultural subsidies and support for domestic industries with a potential for growth. It is also attempting to reimpose tariffs on *salaula*, much of which it claims actually consists of factory seconds and discards that have economic value and so warrant an import tax; and to re-orient its development inwards. "In a sense," two officials recently wrote, "Zambia is now a victim of its own honest policies. Trade in goods and services is now one of the mainstays of the economy, to the detriment of more productive activities and thereby employment opportunities" (Mtonga & Chikoti 2002:5). Or, as one of the Zambians interviewed by Jeter (2002) commented, "The young people really love the [*salaula*] clothes they see…[b]ut is this the way to develop your economy?"

Blaming Chileshe's HIV infection on globalization may be over-simplifying, but it is not fundamentally wrong, although the causal pathways are complicated. Sanjay Basu (2003), in an essay critical of the behaviour change emphasis in HIV prevention programs in Africa, notes, "[T]he top epidemiological predictor for HIV infection around the world is not 'risk behaviour' but rather a low income level"; and average income levels (measured as GDP/per capita) did indeed drop in Zambia and twenty-three other African countries after they opened up their economies to meet IMF/World Bank loan conditions (UN Habitat 2003b:37). In more specific terms, labour markets structured by export demands (notably for minerals) remove men from families and place them in risky working conditions, creating contexts in which the hazards of unsafe sex pale by comparison with the quotidian hazards of the job (Campbell 1997). An actual case study describes evocatively how structural adjustment in Zaire destroyed livelihoods and drastically cut health and education services and employment, creating despondency in many men that led them to increase their own sexually risky behaviours, and eventually forcing many women into selling sex for survival (Schoepf, Schoepf & Millen 2000). "Survival sex" has been described in other African contexts (see e.g. Wojcicki 2002, Wojcicki & Malala 2001), although not always with specific reference to causal pathways from globalization. Finally, the tragic intersection of future economic despair and traditional patriarchy is evident in the practice of some South African men who, discovering they are HIV positive, infect as many others as possible to avoid dying alone (Leclerc-Madlala 1997).

The web of connection between globalization and the HIV pandemic in Africa has many strands. Two of the more important ones so far unexamined are the debt crisis that gave birth to neo-liberal structural adjustment programs, and the politics and adequacy of the aid response by high-income donor nations.

5 Debt, Aid, and Brain Drain

The long-standing 'debt crisis' is a major factor in the inability of low-income countries to sustain or benefit from economic growth (UNCTAD 1999). It is also a major impediment to their ability to invest in health, education, water, sanitation and other essential health infrastructures. For example, in 2001-2002, government expenditure on health services in Bangladesh was $492 million, while expenditure on external debt service was $1.08 billion; and in Kenya, the figure for health spending was $189 million, and for debt repayment $580 million (Rowson & Verheul 2004:8). African countries currently owe more than $15 billion annually in debt servicing charges to rich country creditors, although not all that is actually paid in any given year — an amount that almost equals the total annual value of development assistance they receive (OECD 2004b). Worldwide, the amount of money returned to high-income countries dwarfs the amount they receive in development assistance, creating a 'revolving door' in which what donor countries give in assistance, they receive back multiple times over in debt repayments (Figure 3).

Figure 3. How debt service obligations dwarf development assistance

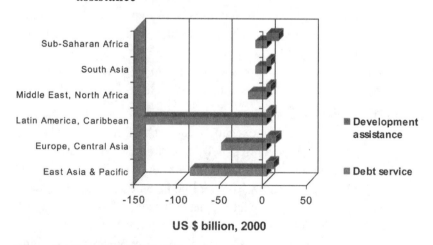

US $ billion, 2000

Source: Pettifor and Greenhill 2002

Journalist Ken Wiwa, the son of Ken Saro-Wiwa, the Nigerian activist hanged for opposing Shell Oil's destruction of his peoples' home-lands, noted bitingly: "You'd need the mathematical dexterity of a forensic accountant to explain why Nigeria borrowed $5 billion, paid back $16 billion, and still owes $32 billion" (Wiwa 2004:A19). The African continent as a whole between 1970 and 2002 borrowed $540 billion, paid back $550 billion and still owes $295 billion (UNCTAD 2004b:19).

The specific causes of debt crises vary from country to country and over time (George 1988, Hanlon 2000, Strange 1998), but it is widely agreed that major contributors include:

- The oil price shocks of 1973 and 1979-80. All countries were affected, but low-income countries in particular had to borrow to pay the costs of suddenly expensive imported oil.

- Profligate lending by banks stuffed with new 'petrodollars,' with few checks on the viability of the loans, or whether the money would simply end up as flight capital.

- The rapid increase in inflation-adjusted interest rates during the early 1980s, resulting from the monetarist policies of the United States. Poor, indebted countries had to borrow more just to keep up with the suddenly very high interest payments alone.

- Devaluation of the local currency (often a requirement of a struc-tural adjustment loan), which doubled or trebled the debt burden, payable in dollars or some other hard currency. This "forc[ed] debtor countries (all except the US) to restructure their economies towards exports with which to earn the hard currency needed to pay for imports and to service debts" (Wade 2002:58).

- Falling world prices for the primary commodities that are the key exports (and foreign exchange earners) of many developing economies.[16] World prices fell for a variety of related reasons: Less demand for them by high-income countries facing recession in the 1980s, oversupply as more low-income countries (often on the advice of lenders eager to have these countries use export earnings for debt repayment) began to produce the same com-modities for export, and oversupply by heavily subsidized high-income commodity producers, especially of agricultural products.

- Capital flight, consisting of two dimensions, which sometimes overlap. In the first, political leaders steal development assistance and other income flows, including bank loans and bribes collected as a cost of doing business, and then hide the assets abroad (see Box 8). In the second, foreign investors and domestic economic elites behave in an economically rational (and usually entirely legal) manner by shifting their assets abroad, usually into hard currencies such as the US dollar, reducing the ability of governments to meet revenue requirements through taxation (Labonte et al. 2004:14-16, 32-34). During 1970-96, "roughly 80 cents on every dollar that flowed into [sub-Saharan Africa] from foreign loans flowed back out as capital flight in the same year" (Ndikumana & Boyce 2003:122); and the economist who coined the phrase "the Washington consensus" to describe the market-oriented axioms that guided development policy in the 1980s has warned that possibilities for progressive taxation to finance social spending in Latin America are limited "because too many of the Latin rich have the option of placing too many of their assets in Miami" (Williamson 2004:13).

BOX 8   Debt, Corruption and the 'Cost' of Doing Business

Transfers of resources to developing countries, as debt relief or direct grants, are increasingly accompanied by requirements that recipient countries demonstrate "good governance", notably by reducing corruption. Superficially the logic of such requirements is unassailable. Transparency International, perhaps the most influential actor in civil society with regard to anti-corruption efforts (Serafini 2004), estimates that just ten of the most notoriously corrupt leaders of the past 20 years, led by Indonesia's Suharto, the Philippines' Marcos and Zaire's Mobutu, embezzled $29-58 billion from some of the poorest countries in the world (Hodess 2004).

The irony of such conditions, however, lies in the routine involvement of Western businesses in a range of corrupt practices. Western businesses in 1999 are said to have paid over $80 billion in bribes to officials in low- and middle-income countries to gain market access (often for weapons purchases) and regulatory relaxation (often in the mining, logging and oil sectors). Such bribes inflate the costs of projects, and may increase the debts of low- and middle-income countries by creating an incentive for leaders to borrow for financially unsustainable but personally lucrative projects (Hawley 2000). Nigeria's vice-president further blames rich nations for allowing corrupt officials to siphon aid funds into private offshore accounts - to the tune, in Nigeria's case, of over $4 billion (Ozoemena 2004).

Multilateral initiatives to control corruption include an OECD Convention on Combating Bribery (which came into force in 1999) and the 2003 UN Convention Against Corruption. The OECD convention has been signed by 35 countries, including a number of middle-income exporters such as South Korea, Chile, Brazil and Turkey as well as members of the OECD. A US review was "generally encouraged" by efforts to implement the convention but concerned about uneven progress (US Department of Commerce 2004).

US leadership in this policy area dates back to the Foreign Corrupt Practices Act, domestic legislation to prohibit bribery of foreign officials by US corporations (McCubbins 2004). Because US firms were thereby placed at a competitive disadvantage, they have and had a strong interest in weakening or circumventing the legislation and, more significantly for our purposes, in supporting multilateral measures like the OECD convention that impose similar constraints on their competitors. US firms clearly take the domestic legislation seriously, especially after recent amendments and sentencing decisions (McCubbins 2004). The director of the Probe International Foundation told a US Congressional committee in 2004 that it was one of the reasons US firms had not been among those indicted in Lesotho for bribing officials to secure contracts for portions of a World Bank-funded dam project. She recommended that national appropriations for the World Bank and other multilateral development banks be made conditional on their implementing the principles embodied in the legislation (Adams 2004).

The effectiveness of the 2003 UN convention is even more uncertain. It potentially, represents a major advance not only because it requires domestic criminalization of various forms of corruption, but also because it specifically addresses the crucial issue of recovery of illegally obtained assets. However, although 113 countries had signed the convention by 2004 (including all the G8), it had been ratified by only 13 (including none of the G8) and 30 ratifications are needed before it comes into force, even with respect to those countries that have ratified it.

Whatever multilateral agreements may be in place, implementation depends on legislation and enforcement at national and sometimes subnational level. Given the asymmetry of power relations in the world economy, it is especially important that industrialized countries both regulate the behaviour of firms under their legal jurisdictions, imposing sanctions that are meaningful when compared with the potential gains from engaging in corruption, and act aggressively to prevent financial institutions from handling proceeds from corruption. Opportunities for legal creativity include national adoption of the principles of the US Foreign Corrupt Practices Act, and further initiatives such as imposing civil and criminal liability on officers, directors and senior managers of institutional investors that own securities of firms found to have violated antibribery statutes in any country party to the international conventions.

The health-damaging effect of debt service obligations, and the structural adjustment conditionalities attached to lending designed primarily around creditors' interests, were well known as early as 1987 (Cornia, Jolly & Stewart, 1987, World Commission on Environment and Development 1987). Not until 1996, after much lobbying by international NGOs, did high-income countries respond in a concerted fashion with the World Bank/IMF Heavily Indebted Poor Country (HIPC) initiative. This quickly became the centrepiece of the industrialized world's debt reduction initiatives, and expanded in 1999 as Enhanced HIPC. It offers partial debt relief to 38 of the world's poorest countries, although not all 38 have actually received such relief. While Enhanced HIPC has led to increases in public spending on such basic needs as health and education in some recipient countries (Gupta et al. 2002), in many the annual cost of debt servicing will still exceed combined spending on health and primary education after they have obtained the maximum debt reduction for which they are eligible (Oxfam 2001). According to one estimate, almost half the HIPC countries' debt will remain unpaid and uncancelled at the conclusion of the initiative (Martin 2004).

This is partly because not enough debt relief has been offered; partly because the resources made available through HIPC may have come at the expense of development assistance flows of other kinds (Killick 2004); and partly because Enhanced HIPC defines a "sustainable" debt load in terms of a present value that is less than 150% of annual export revenues. This criterion, adopted at the insistence of the G7 (Martin 2004), means that some of the world's poorest countries can only rescue themselves from poverty by rapidly increasing the value of their exports. This demand has been described as "internationalized workfare" (Goldstone 2001), an analogy with US welfare reforms that forced mothers into low-wage work on almost any terms (Albelda & Withorn eds. 2001, Tourigny & Jones-Brown eds. 2001). Consider that creditor nations in the EU allow Ghana, a HIPC country, to export raw cocoa for a tariff of just 0.5%. But if Ghana, rather than European-based MNEs, turns the cocoa into chocolate, it faces a tariff of 30.6% (Elliott 2004b). A more defensible criterion for debt relief would first ensure a country had enough money to meet basic human needs, and only then determine how much (if any) of the government budget could be devoted to debt repayment (Pettifor & Greenhill 2002, Greenhill & Sisti 2003).

Debt relief also comes with conditionalities. Poverty reduction has replaced structural adjustment in the official vocabulary of the World Bank and the IMF, but similar macroeconomic policy directions can be observed in the Poverty Reduction Strategy Papers (PRSPs) that are required for HIPC debt relief and, increasingly, for bilateral development assistance or concessional loans from the World Bank. Indeed, policy elements of PRSPs often include "trade-related conditions that are more stringent, in terms of requiring more, or faster, or deeper liberalization, than WTO provisions to which the respective country has agreed" (Brock & McGee 2004:20). There may be democratic benefits in the increased citizen participation that PRSPs urge as important in creating local 'ownership' of a country's poverty reduction strategy, although such participation has so far been tokenistic. But many of the economic conditions associated with PRSPs – notably the "dogmatic demands for privatization and reduced public services" – should be removed (WCSDG 2004:103).[17]

BOX 9 Aircraft, Air Traffic Control and Basic Needs

While the political use of assistance was supposed to decline with the collapse of communism, aid's domestic political and commercial interests persist. In 2002, the Tanzanian government agreed to purchase a £28 million military air traffic control system from Britain's BAE Systems, one of the world's largest defence contractors. BAE Systems actively lobbied for the granting of an export licence for the system, citing the need to preserve 250 jobs in Britain. (Then) international development secretary Clare Short publicly opposed the deal, which was financed by a low interest (concessional) loan from Barclays Bank, after the bank had been granted a lucrative banking licence to operate in Tanzania. Tanzania is a recipient of debt relief under HIPC, eligibility for which precludes the use of concessional loans for military purchases. The World Bank also opposed the loan, arguing that far less expensive systems would be adequate for Tanzania's civilian needs. The loan and purchase nonetheless proceeded, at the Prime Minister's urging. When the cabinet split was publicized, Short temporarily froze £10 million of British aid to Tanzania, as required under HIPC rules, but was ultimately overruled on the issue, and indeed announced a new aid package worth £270 million over six years as the sale went ahead. So did the Tanzanian government's purchase of a £15 million personal jet for the country's president. This case may have been unusual only because such internal disagreements are usually kept out of the public eye, but illuminates the origins of much cynicism about ODA (adapted from Labonte et al. 2004).

ODA is not a panacea for development. Historically, aid has often served the political, strategic or commercial interests of donor nations, particularly so in Africa where "donors have apparently not used recipient governments' revealed commitment to tackling poverty as a basis for country aid allocations," basing assistance instead on "commercial and political considerations" (White & Killick 2001:118).[18] Throughout the developing world, aid is often 'tied' to the purchase of goods and services (in the form of technical cooperation) from donor countries (Labonte et al. 2004:126-129). Similar criticisms are made of debt relief priorities. The USA quickly moved to mobilize international commitments to write off as much as $100 billion of Iraq's debt ($42 billion in write-offs was promised as of December 2004), with some evidence that this is tied to creditors' access to future oil contracts (Dixon 2004). High-income countries have also reportedly used threats of withholding debt relief, ODA and support for loans by the World Bank or IMF to break the growing solidarity amongst low- and middle-income nations in WTO trade (Hilary 2004). Aid has also financed large-scale, environmentally destructive projects with limited relevance to basic needs (Rich 1994, Bosshard et al. 2003), or simply been stolen by corrupt officials (LaFraniere 2004, Vasagar 2004).

Some of these limitations are slowly being removed through commitments to untie aid and provide more aid as sector-wide budget support to government departments. At the same time, aid is increasingly accompanied by conditionalities that parallel those associated with debt relief. The 2003 US commitment to increase its annual aid spending to $15 billion by 2006, by way of its Millennium Challenge Account, makes new funds conditional on "sound economic policies that foster enterprise and entrepreneurship, including more open markets and sustainable budget policies" (UN Secretary-General, 2002 8-9) – in other words, greater market and investment opportunities for US-based firms.

Past and present aid conditionalities have led some activist organizations to promote full debt cancellation rather than more ODA. Debt cancellation, because it provides more autonomy to recipient countries, is preferable to aid, but only if there must be a choice between the two (Birdsall 2002). Simple logic indicates that this is not the case, and simple arithmetic makes it clear that such a tradeoff would be disastrous for the future of much of the developing world. Jubilee Research calculates that at least $16.5 billion per year in new development assistance would be needed in order to ensure that the HIPCs could meet the basic needs of their people, even if their entire external debt were to be cancelled (Pettifor & Greenhill 2002). Jeffrey Sachs and colleagues with the UN Millennium Project estimate that many African countries will require ODA contributions equal to 20-23 per cent of their GDP over the 2004-2015 period if they are to finance achievement of their Millennium Development Goal targets (Sachs et al. 2004:166-167). (See Box 10).

BOX 10 Millennium Development Goals

The Millennium Development Goals (or MDGs) and the associated targets were developed by a working group of several international organizations based on the United Nations General Assembly's Millennium Resolution (Resolution 55/2 19). No binding commitment to implementing the goals exists, but they have become the focus of an unprecedented effort on the part of the World Bank and a variety of agencies within the UN system to measure development progress in a systematic way, and to advocate for additional resources for development with a special emphasis on meeting basic needs. Despite these efforts, two (amongst many) recent assessments conclude that meeting the Goals by the target date of 2015 is unlikely (Sachs et al. 2004; UN Millennium Project 2005). An assessment that focused on the health-related MDGs concluded in December 2003 that: "Even if economic growth accelerates ... and even if progress toward the gender and water goals were to be substantially accelerated, the developing world will wake up on the morning of January 1, 2016 some way from the health targets – Sub-Saharan Africa a long way" (Wagstaff, Claeson et al. 2003:2-12).

The Millennium Development Goals

Goal 1: Eradicate extreme poverty and hunger
Target 1: Halve, between 1990 and 2015, the proportion of people whose income is less than one dollar a day
Target 2: Halve, between 1990 and 2015, the proportion of people who suffer from hunger

Goal 2: Achieve universal primary education
Target 3: Ensure that by 2015 children everywhere, boys and girls alike, will be able to complete a full course of primary schooling

Goal 3: Promote gender equality and empower women
Target 4: Eliminate gender disparity in primary and secondary education preferably by 2005 and to all levels of education no later than 2015

Goal 4: Reduce child mortality
Target 5: Reduce by two-thirds, between 1990 and 2015, the under-five mortality rate

Goal 5: Improve maternal health
Target 6: Reduce by three-quarters, between 1990 and 2015, the maternal mortality ratio

Goal 6: Combat HIV/AIDS, malaria and other diseases
Target 7: Have halted by 2015 and begun to reverse the spread of HIV/AIDS

Target 8: Have halted by 2015 and begun to reverse the incidence of malaria and other major diseases

Goal 7: Ensure environmental sustainability
Target 9: Integrate the principles of sustainable development into country policies and programmes and reverse the loss of environmental resources

Target 10: Halve, by 2015, the proportion of people without sustainable access to safe drinking water and basic sanitation

Target 11: By 2020, to have achieved a significant improvement in the lives of at least 100 million slum dwellers

Goal 8: Develop a global partnership for development
Target 12: Develop further an open, rule-based, predictable, non-discriminatory trading and financial system

Target 13: Address the special needs of the least developed countries

Target 14: Address the special needs of landlocked countries and small island developing states (through the Programme of Action for the Sustainable Development of Small Island Developing States and the outcome of the twenty-second special session of the General Assembly)

Target 15: Deal comprehensively with the debt problems of developing countries through national and international measures in order to make the debt sustainable in the long term

Target 16: In co-operation with developing countries, develop and implement strategies for decent and productive work for youth

Target 17: In co-operation with pharmaceutical companies, provide access to affordable, essential drugs in developing countries

Target 18: In co-operation with the private sector, make available the benefits of new technologies, especially information and communications

The value of ODA as a percentage of most industrialized countries' GNP or GNI, with some notable and laudable exceptions, has been declining since the mid-1980s (Figure 4). The United Nations' 2002 Monterrey Conference on Financing for Development saw donors pledge to raise the inflation-adjusted value of development assistance from $58.2 billion in 2002 to $76.8 billion by 2006. (OECD 2004b:62). This $18 billion increase, a welcome change in direction, nonetheless compares poorly with the additional $40 billion - $70 billion per year in ODA estimated as needed in order to meet the first 7 of the MDGs (Devarajan, Miller & Swanson 2001) – which, by more recent accounts, may be a considerable underestimate (World Bank 2003; UN Millennium Project, 2005). The Commission on Macroeconomics and Health estimated the need for donor financing for health care and health research alone at $27 billion by 2007 – as against total ODA for health of just $8.1 billion in 2002 (Michaud 2003). Thus the gap between what is needed and what is provided is unconscionably vast.

BOX 11 The International Finance Facility

The International Finance Facility (IFF) promoted by the UK (HM Treasury and DFID 2003) is a special case of development financing. It proposes to transform the Monterrey (and subsequent) donor pledges for increased development assistance into bonds, repayable by the donor countries after 2015. The effect of issuing such bonds would be to double the amount of financing available for development within a few years. Coupled with debt cancellation it would bring international development financing closer to the estimates of the amount needed by low- and middle-income countries to meet their MDG targets.

The IFF proposal was first raised at the 2003 G8 Evian summit as one of several possible financing instruments. Economic analyses conclude that this sudden increase in development assistance is not beyond the absorptive capacity of recipient countries (Mavrotas 2003). Almost 40 countries and numerous development agencies and NGOs support the proposal, which has been less warmly received by donor nations (Lister, Ingram & Prowle 2004). The concerns include the following.

- It depends on additional pledges of increased aid by donors and, at present, would not bind them to participation in future pledging rounds.
- Repayments by donor countries could compromise the objective of meeting or sustaining aid levels at 0.7% of GNI after 2015.
- A governance structure would have to be developed that did not simply follow the preferences of individual donors/lenders for disbursement of aid.
- It could add another layer of administrative complexity to an already crowded field, especially when an increase in funding available as grants through the World Bank could achieve a similar outcome (Rogerson, Hewitt & Waldenberg 2004). If this option were followed, however, Bank grants and lending would have to come with fewer or no conditionalities apart from financial accountability.
- Perhaps most importantly, the IFF as now proposed incorporates strongly market-oriented conditionalities, such as "sequenced opening up of markets to global trade" and "improving the environment to encourage private sector-led growth" (HM Treasury & DFID 2003).
- The health implications of such requirements are contested, and have proved to be highly destructive in the past. The claim that in the last 40 years those developing countries that have been more open, and traded more in the world economy, have seen faster growth rates than those that have remained closed is disputed by many development economists, notably with respect to its confusion of correlation with causation.

These concerns do not negate the potential usefulness of the IFF, but they must be addressed if the proposal is to be meaningful as a contribution to improving global health equity. It is also important to put both its rationale and its equity impacts into context. A 2004 IFF media update says donors are committed to reaching the aid target of 0.7%, an overstatement in the case of the USA, which has never agreed to this target, "but a number have fiscal constraints that will not allow them to increase aid levels in the short to medium term". This essentially means that G7 governments are unwilling (or unable, because of the anticipated electoral consequences of tax revolt) to raise revenues that are trivial relative to the incomes of their citizens, even when the Commission on Macroeconomics and Health says they could save at *least eight million lives a year by 2010. It should further be noted that these "fiscal constraints" are invoked against a background of huge increases in US military expenditures subsequent to the invasion of Iraq; tax cuts favouring wealthy individuals and corporations, especially in the USA where the value of President Bush's tax cuts for the wealthiest 1 per cent of the population (average annual income just under $1 million) over the period 2001-2010 will amount to $689 billion, in contrast to only $23 billion going to the lowest income quintile (Citizens for Tax Justice 2002, 2003). Added to this is the failure of G8 countries to close tax havens which are estimated to cost the UK treasury many billions of pounds in annual tax revenue (Campbell 2004) and the US treasury $10-20 billion a year in corporate taxes alone (McIntyre & Nguyen 2004).*

Finally, assuming a 5% bond interest rate, the IFF would disburse $500 billion in additional aid until 2015, at a cost of $720 billion over the repayment period (HM Treasury & DFID 2003). Since bond investors tend to be the ultra-rich, the $220 billion in interest earnings would most likely go to those individuals or corporate investors whose lower tax rates and easier access to tax avoidance largely created the "fiscal constraints" that the UK treasury and department for international development argue necessitate the creation of the IFF in the first place.

Figure 4. Trends in G7 development assistance, with selected comparison countries

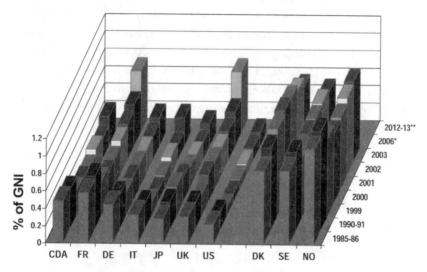

* Assuming all commitments made at Monterrey in 2002 are fulfilled (G7 only)
** Promised (France and UK only)
Sources: Chirac 2003; MacAskill 2004; OECD 2005.

We cannot leave Chileshe's story without discussing another of globalization's health-damaging effects: the "global conveyor belt" that is seeing high-income countries, which once mined low-income nations for their natural resources, now recruiting their human resources (Chen et al 2004, Schrecker and Labonte 2004). Amongst the increasing flow of 'brain drain' migrants are physicians and nurses. Canada, the UK and the USA are the major beneficiary countries.[19] Not only does this deprive countries facing the world's most severe health crises of needed human resources – sub-Saharan Africa, for example, is estimated to need 1 million more health workers to meet its peoples' health needs (Chen et al. 2004) – it also represents an economic transfer (in the form of training costs) from poor to rich. Across all low- and middle-income countries, the annual subsidy to the health systems of the affluent OECD countries amounts to over $500 million (Ndiaye 2003).

Solutions to this problem will not be easy. Probably the only viable solution, despite the obvious political difficulties, is a multilateral convention on migration of health professionals that recognizes the losses to poorer countries and compensates these in some fashion. One might imagine a migration policy whereby, for every health professional accepted by a high-income from a low-income country, a population-weighted number of unskilled migrants similarly seeking to immigrate would also be accepted. Such an approach, according to the World Bank's David Dollar (2002:33), "would help [high-income countries] with their own looming labour shortages, improve living standards in sending countries, and reduce the growing illegal human trade [of unskilled workers] with all of its abuses."[20]

So far we have examined the dominant globalization › growth › wealth › health story, and found it wanting. One point we have made is that the collapse of African economies and health systems is partly explained by the fact that countries in the region opened their economies to global competition without adequate ways to handle the consequent social and economic dislocations, and in some cases facing active hostility from international lending agencies to using the resources and policy instruments they did have. The story of Antonia and her father brings the issue of global trade rules as potential health threats into sharper focus.

Their story begins with land reforms in Mexico a century earlier that created subsistence and smallholding production plots. These plots were big enough to feed a family and earn some income by selling to local markets, but did not provide (and were never intended to provide) economies of scale like those of modern corporate farming practices. In the run-up to the North American Free Trade Agreement (NAFTA), the Mexican government ended its subsidies to "small-scale producers of basic crops" including corn (Preibisch, Rivera Herrejon & Wiggins 2002), the key ingredient in *tortillas*, Mexico's staple food. When NAFTA opened the Mexico-US border, corn from the United States, where large-scale agribusiness is massively and unapologetically subsidized, flooded the Mexican market.[21] Currency crises and IMF conditional loans also played a role in the rapid decline of Mexico's corn prices. Following the financial crisis that led to the collapse of the peso in 1995, the bailout organized by the Clinton administration included a $1 billion export credit that obligated Mexico to purchase US corn. Predictably, Mexican imports of US corn to Mexico rose by 120 percent in just one year (Carlsen 2003:2-3).

Mexican corn production stagnated while prices declined (Henriques & Patel 2004). Small farmers were hardest hit, becoming much poorer than they were in the early 1990s (Condesa Consulting Group 2004:2), despite subsequent efforts by the Mexican government to re-introduce some of the subsidies they had originally removed

(*Bridges* 2002b). Some 700,000 agricultural jobs disappeared over the same period. The lack of demand for farm labour depressed wages to such an extent that, in 2001, a Mexican farm worker earned less, in real terms, than half what she or he made twenty years earlier (Condesa Consulting Group 2004:5). Unsurprisingly, Mexico's rural poverty rates rose to over 70 per cent; the minimum wage lost over 75 per cent of its purchasing power; infant mortality rates for the poor increased; and wage inequalities became the most severe of those in Latin America (Lichfield 2000, Schwartz 2002). Between 1984, when Mexico's 1982 debt crisis led to one of the first and most wrenching programs of lender-driven economic adjustment, and 2000 the share of national income flowing to the poorest decile of the population fell from 1.7 per cent to 1.5 per cent, while the share of the richest decile increased from 32.8 per cent to 38.7 per cent (Schwarz 2002:155). Adding insult to injury, as corn prices fell, the price of commercially marketed *tortillas* rose by almost 300 per cent – because just two companies produce 97 per cent of all the corn-products in Mexico (Henriques & Patel 2004). Apparently to ensure a cheap corn supply for these two companies, the Mexican government chose not to avail itself of NAFTA approved tariff quotas and extended phase-in periods that would have severely limited the quantity of US corn crossing the border; or to collect permissible tariffs on US corn imports that cost its public treasury over $2 billion in foregone revenues since 1994 (Henriques & Patel 2004).

Conventional economic theories, and conventional economists, have little sympathy for producers like Miguel, dismissing them as "inefficient incumbents facing increased foreign competition" (Rugman & Verbeke 2003:96). Miguel and his family, on this account, should move to the city and join an expanding pool of dispossessed, low-cost labour, or else reinvent themselves as agricultural exporters.

We have already seen the downside of the first option. As for the second, even if some agricultural producers manage to make the transition to successful exporting, the implications of organizing an economy around such transitions are not altogether benign. Post-NAFTA, Mexico did expand its exports of fruits and legumes to the USA (Condesa Consulting Group 2004). Agricultural production also rose, despite the huge drop in prices and farm worker employment that, ironically, indicated some improvement in efficiency and productivity (Carlsen 2003, Condesa Consulting Group 2004). But these relatively small gains came with a potentially high cost: an increase in Mexico's 'food dependence,' as its food imports began to grow rapidly (Condesa Consulting Group 2004). This pattern follows classical economic theory that holds that, as a country's food exports rise on commodities where it has comparative advantage, the income it generates allows it to import the food it can no longer grow and where it may not be competitive. Unfortunately, this is not always how things work out in practice. According to a report by the Interhemispheric Resource Centre: "While President Fox and his cabinet boast of six billion pesos in agro-export earnings, farmers point out that that money went into the pockets of fewer than 7 percent of Mexico's farmers" (Carlsen 2003:5). If most of these revenues were re-directed into purchasing Mexican produced goods or invested in Mexican enterprise, thus providing more income and jobs for workers and enabling them to afford food imports, the classical theory would hold. But it is highly unlikely this is the case.

Nor is Mexico's experience unique. As food exports from low-income countries rise, food security often declines (FAO 1996, Karl 1997), especially for the poor. Thus, many low-income countries are pressing for a 'food security' exception to trade liberalization requirements under the WTO's Agreement on Agriculture – a criterion agreed to in principle by WTO members. However, details must still be negotiated and subjected to the political arm-twisting of trade talks (*Bridges* 2004b). A development strategy organized around agricultural exports can also add to environmental stress, as subsistence farming moves to marginal and ecologically sensitive land to make way for export crops in the fertile areas. Irrigation demands and toxic fertilizer/pesticide run-offs can compromise access to potable water, especially in water-scarce regions in Africa (UNEP 1999, Worldwatch Institute 2001). There are gendered impacts, too, as the decline in domestic food availability increases women's labour time in household food production (Tibaijuka 1994) even as export earnings accrue primarily to (relatively few) men who dominate the agricultural export sector in most low- and middle-income countries (Woodward 1996).

These dilemmas are intractable, but not insoluble. And capturing the economic gains of agricultural export earnings can lead to widely shared improvements in health. But the outcome depends on how equitably benefits are allocated amongst all citizens. This condition, in turn, requires taxation, regulatory and management capacities that exceed those in all low- and most middle-income countries. Globalization may actually reduce the extent to which national and sub-national governments can develop such capacities, if its winners can form a politically decisive coalition (which need represent only a minority of the population) in support of regressive taxation, low levels of public social provision, highly selective regulation and strong support for property rights.

Miguel's situation illustrates the precarious future of small agricultural producers worldwide exposed to competition from larger countries with fatter wallets to subsidize their own agroindustries. It is atypical in two respects: first, it results in the first instance from measures by the Mexican government (starting in the mid-1980s) to accelerate the country's integration into the global economy; second, the relevant trade rules are part of a regional rather than a global trade agreement. While NAFTA still gets a lot of attention in the Americas, more attention worldwide has been paid to the impacts of the agreements administered by the World Trade Organization (WTO).

Globalization, Health and the World Trade Organization

The WTO was formed in 1995 at the conclusion of the Uruguay Round of talks on the General Agreement on Tariffs and Trade (GATT). Unlike most multilateral agreements, the 29 administered by WTO provide for a dispute settlement procedure (under the auspices of WTO) backed up by enforcement provisions in the form of fines or monetized trade concessions. Any of the 147 member countries (as of September, 2004) can launch a complaint against other members they think are failing to live up to their WTO commitments. Key principles underpinning all WTO agreements are *national treatment* (foreign goods, investment or services are treated the same as domestic ones), *most favoured nation* (whatever special preferences are given to one trading partner must be given to all WTO member nations) and *least trade restrictive practices* (whatever environmental or social regulations a country adopts domestically must be those that least impede trade).

BOX 12 Special and Differential Treatment

"Uniform rules for unequal partners can only produce unequal outcomes" WCSDG 2004:85).

Special and differential treatment (SDT) has been a feature of the world trading system since the beginning of the GATT, and holds more potential than agreement-specific exceptions for "levelling the playing field" between rich and poor member nations. The differing size, economic power, wealth, development level and interests of WTO member-nations demands agreement on how these divergences will be managed if a multilateral trading system is to have political and functional legitimacy (South Centre 1999). SDT also bears indirectly but powerfully on health if it enables poverty-reducing economic growth.

With the birth of the WTO, SDT suffered a "massive dilution" (Das 2000:8). Under the earlier GATT, SDT meant a lower degree of obli-

gation by low- and middle-income countries, a principle referred as 'nonreciprocity,' meaning that such countries did not have to implement trade agreements in the same way as did high-income nations. Under the WTO, it now simply means a longer time frame to fulfill all obligations of most agreements. Moreover, many SDT provisions in the new WTO agreements are written in "best endeavour" language that "calls on," but does not require, members to take the development needs of poorer countries into account (Jawara & Kwa 2003:12,47). Intense lobbying by poorer African and Asian nations led to inclusion in the Doha Ministerial Declaration (WTO 2001a) of a commitment to review "all Special and Differential provisions...with a view to strengthening them and making them more precise, effective and operational" (44, emphasis added). WTO members, however, disagree over what "strengthening" means. Low- and middle-income countries want to modify many agreements to make them more supportive of health and development objectives, partly by granting them more policy flexibility (Keck & Low 2004). Most high-income countries oppose this (Bridges 2002a). And even though the Doha ministerial mandated members to identify "best endeavour" SDT measures and "to consider the legal and practical implications ... of converting them into mandatory provisions" (WTO Doha Decision on Implementation-Related Decision and Concerns 12(i), 2001), no progress was made by the July 2002 deadline, and little progress since (Keck & Low 2004, Bridges 2004b).

The politics of SDT are complex. Should exemptions be permitted by graduated time (as is presently the case); by defining eligibility (Brazil, Mexico and India are quite different from Bolivia, Nicaragua and Bangladesh); by country-specific economic thresholds (such as $1,000/per capita, below which WTO members are presently allowed to provide export subsidies on manufactured goods); or by development-need (argued on a case by case basis) (Keck & Low 2004)? Each option is flawed. Time alone does not determine need. Agreeing on an eligibility definition flies in the face of developing world solidarity. Aggregate economic thresholds hide important non-economic development needs affected by trade agreements, such as gender rights, environmental protections and food security. And who would adjudicate the individual case-arguments?

> *At base, the WTO struggle over SDT is between poorer countries and analysts who frame SDT in the language of political and human rights, a stance more in keeping with public health history and practice; and high-income countries and analysts who view politicization as unhelpful, and to be avoided through provision-specific criteria tied to neoliberal economic theories.*

Several WTO agreements have specific bearing on the pathways linking globalization and health, and deserve further discussion.

The *Agreement on Sanitary and Phytosanitary Measures* (SPS) requires that a country's food and drug safety regulations be based on a scientific risk assessment, *even if* the regulations do not differentiate between domestic and imported products (Drache et al. 2002). Canada, the USA and Brazil initiated a WTO dispute to force the EU to accept imports of hormone-treated beef. The EU does not allow the use of these hormones on its cattle. There is also evidence that these hormones may cause cancer in animals. The WTO dispute panel concluded that the EU failed to conduct a proper scientific risk assessment proving that hormones were a human health risk. The WTO dispute panel rejected as inadequate the scientific arguments presented to them by the EU, including evidence of possible, though not definitive, human carcinogenicity provided by the International Agency for Research on Cancer (Charnovitz 2001, Sullivan & Shainblum 2001).

The EU still does not allow hormone-treated beef into its countries, and is paying millions of dollars each year to the complaining countries (the United States and Canada) in compensating trade sanctions. The European Commission in November 2004 filed its own complaint against the continuing trade sanctions, arguing that its growth hormone legislation is now based on a full scientific risk assessment and so no longer violates the SPS agreement (*Bridges* 2004c). At the same time, however, the SPS can be used in ways that arguably discriminate unfairly against developing countries. The European Union has imposed a substantially tougher standard for aflatoxin in dried fruits and nuts than any other nation, resulting in an anticipated loss of $670 million per year in agricultural export revenues for African countries (Otsuki, Wilson & Sewadeh 2001). If global health equity is to be an outcome, some reasonable compromise needs to be struck between a country's sovereign right to the highest level of precautionary health protection and the financial inability of low-income countries to abide by extremely stringent regulations.

The *Technical Barriers to Trade Agreement* (TBT) requires that all domestic regulations be "least trade restrictive," treat "like products" the same and be higher than international standards only if they can be justified on specific health grounds. Canada used this agreement to argue that France's ban on the use of asbestos products was discriminatory since asbestos was "like" the glass fibre insulation France allowed. Canada lost this case – the only instance in which WTO mechanisms have favoured health over trade – because of the enormous amount of scientific evidence for the cancer-causing properties of asbestos (WTO 2000).[22] Such conclusive evidence is rarely available. Both the TBT and the SPS instantiate 'trade-creep': a process in which trade rules limit how national governments can regulate their domestic health and environment affairs even if they treat products from other countries no differently than their own – that is, even if they honour the principle of 'national treatment' (Drache et al. 2002).

The *Agreement on Trade-Related Investment Measures* (TRIMS) prevents countries from attaching performance requirements (such as minimum levels of local content) to approvals of foreign investment. Such requirements have proved useful in the development of a viable domestic economy, partly by ensuring health-promoting employment and income adequacy for marginalized groups or regions. Their removal benefits investors from high-income countries much more than it does people living within low- and middle-income nations (Greenfield 2001).

Similarly the *Agreement on Government Procurement* (AGP) requires governments to take into account only "commercial considerations" when making purchasing decisions, precluding preferences based on environment, human or labour rights. Although this is a voluntary agreement that few low- or middle-income countries have signed, high-income countries are intent on making it mandatory and binding on all WTO members as part of their agenda for the Doha round of negotiations, begun in 2001.

BOX 13   NAFTA, the FTAA and the Right of Companies to Sue Governments

The WTO is not the only free trade regime with implications for government regulatory capacity or provision of essential public services. The North American Free Trade Area (NAFTA) and the proposed Free Trade Area of the Americas (FTAA) also have potentially profound health effects. NAFTA has a particularly problematic section, Chapter 11, which permits private foreign companies to deny democratically elected governments the ability to regulate in the public health interests of their citizens.

The following illustrations relate to Canada. The Canadian government let its legislation for plain packaging of tobacco products die after representatives of Phillip Morris International and R.J. Reynolds Tobacco International argued that it constituted an expropriation of assets, violating NAFTA investment and intellectual property obligations. The Canadian government similarly repealed its ban of the gasoline additive MMT, a known neurotoxin, and paid $13 million in compensation after Ethyl Corporation argued, again on the strength of the NAFTA investment Chapter 11, that the ban had the effect of expropriating its assets even if there was no "taking" in the classic understanding of expropriation. Both these NAFTA challenges achieved their goal of overturning a public health measure, although neither went to a dispute panel. More recently, a US-based water company is using NAFTA to sue the Canadian province of British Columbia for $10.5 billion due to restrictions on bulk water exports legislated by the government. The declared intent of Canadian federal and provincial governments to prohibit international trade in water (primarily to the US) may be in violation of NAFTA (Shrybman 1999); states bordering the Great Lakes are currently drafting legislation to permit commercial diversion of water from the basin despite Canada's opposition, arguing that NAFTA gives them the right to do so. Of course, Canadian companies have also used Chapter 11 to challenge regulations in the US. Methanex Corporation, a Canadian-based producer of the gasoline additive MTBE, a suspect carcinogen, is suing for $970 million because California banned its use in 1999. Of 39 such Chapter 11 suits filed *to January 1, 2005, 6 have been dismissed, 10 are under tribunal investigation, 15 are pending and the rest have been withdrawn or settled 'out of court' (Sinclair 2005). Total damages against Canada: $27 million; against Mexico: $18 million; against the USA: $0 (Sinclair 2005).*

With respect to health care, NAFTA provides that governments can expropriate foreign-owned investments only for a public purpose and if they provide compensation. This opens the door to NAFTA claims that measures to expand public health insurance in Canada (where prescription drugs, home care and dental care are currently privately insured), or to restrict private for-profit provision of health care services, amount to expropriation and that compensation must be paid to US or Mexican investors who are adversely affected.

From a health vantage point, NAFTA's Chapter 11 should be rescinded. Article 15 of the Chapter on Investment in the agreement on the FTAA, which would similarly allow investor-state suits, should be deleted. And no such provision should ever be adopted in the multilateral agreements administered by the WTO.

TABLE 1: Health Impacts of Selected Trade Agreements

Agreement	Health Impacts from Loss of Domestic Regulatory Space
Agreement on Trade Related Intellectual Property Rights	Extends patent protection rights, limiting governments' abilities to provide essential medicines at affordable costs. Higher cost of drugs with extended patent protection drains money useful for primary health care. Case example: Access to antiretroviral drugs.
Agreement on Sanitary and Phytosanitary Measures	Requires scientific risk assessments even when foreign goods are treated no differently than domestic goods (i.e., even when there is no discrimination between a domestic and a foreign supplier of the good). Such assessments are costly, and are imperfect in assessing the many potential health risks associated with environmental and manufactured products. Case example: The successful challenge to the European Union's ban on the use of artificial hormones in raising beef.
Technical Barriers to Trade Agreement	Requires that any regulatory barrier to the free flow of goods be 'least trade restrictive as possible.' Many trade disputes over domestic health and safety regulations have invoked this agreement. The only WTO dispute where the health exception, allowing countries to abrogate from trade agreement rules for purposes of protecting human, animal and environmental health was in favour of France's ban on the import of Canadian asbestos products. This occurred under appeal, and followed widespread negative reaction to the initial WTO ruling in favour of Canada.
Agreement on Trade Related Investment Measures	Limits countries' abilities to direct investment where it would do most good for domestic economic development and employment equity, both of which are important to improving population health.
Agreement on Government Procurement	Limits governments' abilities to give priority to domestic firms bidding on its contracts, or to require purchases of goods from local companies, both of which can promote employment opportunities and regional equity, which in turn have strong links to better population health. This is currently an 'optional' agreement to which few developing countries have 'signed on.'
Agreement on Agriculture	Continuing export and producer subsidies by the US, EU, Japan and Canada depress world prices and cost developing countries hundreds of millions of dollars in lost revenue which could be used to fund health, education and other health-promoting services. Subsidized food imports from wealthy countries undermine domestic growers' livelihoods. Market barriers to food products from developing countries persist and deny poorer countries trade-related earnings.

The *Agreement on Agriculture* was designed to increase global trade in agricultural goods by reducing tariffs and phasing out export subsidies (financial assistance for food exports) and production subsidies (financial assistance for farmers). During a ten-year moratorium on trade challenges under this Agreement that only ended December 31, 2004, many high-income countries failed to reduce their tariffs on agricultural products (World Bank/IMF 2002, Watkins 2002), and retained both tariff peaks (a higher-than-average import tax) on raw food imports and tariff escalations on finished food products (where more money can be made), taxing them at 2 – 3 times the rate of raw food imports (Watkins 2002). High-income countries also continued to pay huge subsidies to their domestic agricultural producers. Failure to reach an agreement on subsidy removal was the main reason for the collapse of the Cancún WTO ministerial talks in 2003. An August 2004 WTO 'framework agreement' to begin phasing out subsidies may remedy this impasse, but details are still subject to negotiation and the USA has stated it will not begin to negotiate such reductions until *after* developing countries lower their agricultural tariffs (*Bridges* 2004a). Incredibly, the August 2004 agreement allows the USA to retain a $180 billion increase in domestic farm subsidies announced in 2002, as long as it can show that they do not affect current levels of agricultural production (*Bridges* 2004b).

Figure 5: Rich world agricultural subsidies in perspective

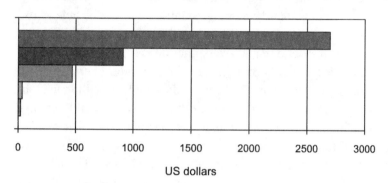

US dollars

■ Japan annual dairy subsidy, per cow
■ EU annual dairy subsidy, per cow
□ Per capita annual income, sub-Saharan Africa
□ Per capita cost of package of essential health interventions
□ Per capita annual health expenditure, 63 low income countries

Sources: Commission on Macroeconomics and Health (2001), United Nations Development Programme (2003) and World Bank data.

The *Agreement on Trade-Related Intellectual Property Rights* (TRIPS) is unlike other WTO agreements in that it does not 'free' trade, but protects intellectual property rights, mostly (at the moment) held by companies or individuals in rich countries.   Health concerns about TRIPS center on the role of extended patent protection on access to anti-retrovirals or other essential drugs.   This debate is now temporarily muted, after prolonged campaigns by many low-income country governments and civil society organizations resulted in the November, 2001 *Declaration on TRIPS and Public Health* (World Trade Organization 2001a) and a subsequent interpretation by the WTO General Council in August 2003 ('t Hoen 2002, Sell 2003:146-162, WTO 2003).   Despite resistance on the part of some high-income countries, especially the USA, the *Declaration* and its interpretation established that health concerns could justify both compulsory licensing (enabling production of lower cost generic versions of patented drugs) and production of generics for export to countries that lack domestic production capacity ("parallel imports," in WTO-speak).   Nonetheless, the USA is now using bilateral trade agreements to create 'TRIPS-plus' clauses that undermine the *Declaration*, with the intent of 'ratcheting

61

up' such clauses into regional trade agreements (WCSDG 2004). Concern also remains that developing countries will not be able to use the August 2003 WTO interpretation of the *Declaration* because it places so many restrictions and oversights on the use of compulsory licensing that, in the words of a leader with the India Pharmaceutical Association, "no generic manufacturer would be able or willing to comply with its provisions" (cited in Jawara, Kwa & Sharma 2004:xxxiii). Meanwhile Canada, the first G7 country to change its domestic legislation to allow domestic firms to produce generic copies of patented drugs for export to developing countries, was simultaneously lauded for its leadership and criticized for the small number of drugs initially covered under the legislative amendments (Elliot 2004, Orbinski 2004).

Finally, the *General Agreement on Trade in Services* (GATS) is a complex framework agreement introduced at the conclusion of the Uruguay Round; national commitments under GATS continue to be negotiated. GATS was pushed onto the GATT agenda by the high-income countries because of rapid growth in the economic value of services in domestic commerce and global trade (Sinclair 2000). It was conceived, and continues to be defended, primarily as a vehicle for the expansion of business opportunities for multinational service corporations (Hilary 2001), almost all of which are based in high-income countries, and are constantly on the lookout for new opportunities. Service businesses covered by GATS that have connections with health and health determinants include health care itself, health insurance[23], education, and water and sanitation services (Sanger 2001, Pollock & Price 2003, SEATINI & EQUINET 2004).

Some commentators argue that whether reducing barriers to trade and investment in such services is good or bad for population health depends on the domestic regulatory structures put in place (Adlung & Carzaniga 2003). However, the World Health Organization's 2000 *World Health Report* cautioned that "few countries (with either high or low income) have developed adequate strategies to regulate the private financing and provision of health services" and that "the harm caused by market abuses is difficult to remedy after the fact" (WHO 2000:125). The same caution should be applied to education, and especially to water and sanitation – an area in which many privatization experiences of the last decade have generated intense political resistance because of their predictably negative effects on the poor and economically insecure (Loftus & McDonald 2001, McDonald 2002, Shaffer, Brenner & Yamin 2002, Budds & McGranahan 2003).

GATS does not directly drive privatization, but functions as a trap-door that locks in existing (and future) levels of private provision of services. It may also indirectly create incentives for foreign investors and their actual or prospective host country joint-venture partners to lobby for privatization, because of the security it provides for investments in newly privatized services. The GATS exception for "a [government] service which is supplied neither on a commercial basis, nor in competition with one or more service suppliers" (Article 1:3b) is often cited as evidence that concern over privatization is misplaced. This clause, however, may collapse under an eventual challenge, since most countries allow some commercial or competitive provision of virtually all public services (Pollock & Price 2000, Sinclair 2000). There is further concern that Mode 4 of GATS (which applies to the 'temporary' movement of service workers between countries) could exacerbate the present 'brain drain' of health professionals to jurisdictions where they can earn more money and enjoy better working conditions. It is often argued in defence of Mode 4 that exporting countries will benefit from the remittances such workers send home. But remittances represent private, not public, gains; they go to family members of the offshore worker and may accrue largely to affluent households, thus worsening income inequalities in the exporting country.

Finally, GATS commits all WTO members to a "progressively higher level of liberalization" in all service sectors (Article XIX). This provision, shared with several other WTO agreements, prevents countries from withdrawing, without penalty, from market access commitments. This means that such commitments will effectively lock in privatization, making it extremely costly for governments to reverse commitments to allow commercial provision – for instance, of health care or health insurance.

BOX 14 Globalization, Privatization and Health Care

When considering privatization in health care, a distinction should be made between provision and financing. In almost all countries some health care is publicly financed, but it may be delivered either publicly (e.g. through hospitals that are part of the UK National Health Service) or privately (e.g. by doctors who bill Canadian provincial health insurance plans for the services they provide, but are not government employees). Privatization of both financing and delivery is increasing worldwide, particularly in Latin America, and often with the prodding of the World Bank and IMF. Regardless of the type of intervention, most World Bank and Inter-American Development Bank initiatives "have favoured the private financing and provision of health care over the former public financing and provision that predominated in most Latin American countries" (Armada, Mutaner & Navarro 2001).

There are evocative examples of how such privatization creates inequalities in access. Between 1974 and 1989 total private health care expenditures in Chile rose substantially while public health care expenditures declined (Collins & Lear 1995). Many poor people were left with under-funded, low quality public health care. Although public health expenditures have been increasing since the return of democratic regimes in 1990, growth in private health care expenditures in Chile still outstrips that for public health care (Leon 2002), and foreign companies now provide 60% of Chile's health insurance (Wasserman & Cornejo 2002). In Brazil, private health care provides 120,000 doctors and 370,000 hospital beds to the richest 25% of the population, while the public system has just 70,000 doctors and 565,000 hospital beds for the remaining 75% (Zarrilli 2002a).

A recent study of the effects of structural adjustment programmes in eight low and middle-income countries (Haddad & Mohindra 2001) found that even if the poor are still disadvantaged, inequalities in access have been reduced in countries such as Colombia, Thailand and to some extent Mexico who have been more proactive in trying to improve access to the poor. The picture is different in the four African countries studied, Burkina Faso, Uganda, Kenya and Zimbabwe. More specifically:

- *Classical "hard" liberal adjustments have been clearly harmful in countries such as Kenya and Zimbabwe, and the poor paid the price.*

- *Cost recovery is invariably a barrier for the poor, even in countries where revenues of cost recovery have been reinjected into the system (such as Burkina Faso or Uganda). Cost recovery is a regressive policy, and also apparently not a very efficient mechanism to raise revenues.*

- *Few studied countries have really privatized their health systems but, as part of health sector reform, most have removed regulations limiting the development of the private market. As a result, they have experienced a strong (and often anarchic) growth of the private sector. In several places and especially in urban contexts, the private sector is now dominant in terms of health care utilization, a process facilitated by the general and often dramatic deterioration of the quality of care in the public sector.*

- *Public facilities do not work well and are unpopular almost everywhere. They offer poor quality services; personnel are often unmotivated and rude. By contrast, although private sector services are not necessarily of high quality, they are usually much more appreciated by the public than those supplied by government institutions (Slim Haddad, Université de Montréal, personal communication, December 2004)*

Another effect of these trends is a decline in political support for universal public programmes from higher-income earners, in favour of private health care and insurance. In some countries this is actively supported by tax incentives to higher-income earners to purchase private health care coverage or education. Yet private provision of health care (and of education and other essential public goods) is less efficient, often less effective and always more inequitable than public, risk-pooling programmes. And health care is not like other commercial services. Public systems for its provision, or at least for its financing, arose precisely because private systems proved inadequate and inequitable.

BOX 15 Water Privatization and the GATS

Water and sanitation services historically were largely provided by the public sector. Only in the past two decades has a large, oligopolistic private sector in these services arisen, primarily the result of macroeconomic policies of "privatisation and de-regulation aimed at encouraging private participation in water and waste management projects" (Bisset et al. 2003:5). Many of these policies arose as part of IMF/World Bank loan conditions. A review of IMF loan agreements across 40 countries during 2000 found that privatization or full-cost recovery was a condition of 12 of them (cited in Hilary 2001). A third (N = 84) of World Bank water supply loans during the 1990s require some form of privatization, and the pace of such requirements is increasing. Fifty-eight per cent of short-term structural adjustment loans between 1996 and 1999 had privatization as a condition; over 80 per cent of all Bank-funded water projects in 2002 did the same (Centre for Public Integrity 2003). This has particularly been the case in Latin America, where the bulk of private participation in water services in low- and middle-income countries is located.

Water privatization programs in the capital of Mauritania led to water costs consuming over one-fifth of total average household budgets for low-income families (World Bank findings cited in Hilary 2001); and to thousands of households being cut off of privatized water delivery systems in South Africa, leading to a deadly outbreak of cholera (Bond 2003). Latin American water privatization schemes have been tried, and failed, in Puerto Rico (1995-1999), Trinidad (1994-1998), Argentina (1995-1998) and several other countries. In each case, rates skyrocketed, service was sporadic or inefficient, huge deficits were created and, in most instances, the contracts were not renewed or the providers simply walked away (Shaffer, Brenner & Yamin 2002). There is considerable concern that the GATS agreement could be used to open up private trade in and increased privatization of water. If this were to occur, the reversal of the hugely unpopular water privatization scheme in Cochabamba, Bolivia, following popular riots, could not have been undertaken without massive compensation paid to foreign water supply companies. Forty countries have committed to liberalize environmental services under GATS, including 26 low- and middle-

income countries (WTO Services Database Online). Such liberalization could lead to increased privatization in the provision of water.

Public water provision is not always a guarantee of access or fairness in financing. In many developing countries, more affluent neighbourhoods enjoy water access through the public piped system, while those residing in poorer slums often purchase bottled water from informal suppliers at unit prices 10- or 20-times higher (Bisset et al. 2003:26). Tariff hikes for those already connected to piped water and debit cards for the poor are frequently advised as strategies, in the first instance to fund extensions of piped water to poor communities (McIntosh 2003) and, in the second, to allow the presumably less expensive piped water (compared to bottled or local well water) to be purchased when families can afford it (Sullivan 2003). This may increase availability for poorer families or slums. But unless progressive forms of taxation to fund water infrastructure accompany these strategies, which allow for extensive cross-subsidization from rich to poor, the equity, access and fair financing health systems and right to health principles will not be met, nor will any of those associated with public health.

Let us return to Miguel's daughter, Antonia. Her asthma is unlikely to be treated, because Mexico's "fragmented health care sector" (Schwartz 2002:165), despite recent improvements, still leaves half of its population without access to health insurance (Barraza-Llorens et al. 2002). Her asthma may also result from exposure to air pollution from manufacturing operations in the neighbouring *maquiladora,* or to exhaust emissions from trucks taking its products north to the USA. Even with the recent loss of more than 300 manufacturing plants to China (Anon 2003), northern Mexico remains home to over 3,000 manufacturing plants producing goods ranging from furniture and car parts to electronic components and textiles. As costs for pollution control and health and safety standards rose in the USA, and with the establishment of the NAFTA, many of the more hazardous and polluting links in the industrial production chain moved to the *maquiladoras* (Frey 2003) – reflecting the market-driven rationality that underpins neoliberal economics. A review of research on the environmental and occupational hazards associated with the *maquiladoras* documents increased ground water and air pollution and the often-illegal discharge of highly toxic chemicals (Frey 2003). Despite a higher than average income level (Schwartz 2002), northern Mexico has higher than average rates of infant and age-adjusted mortality, and increased rates of mortality and morbidity for infectious disease partly due to the rapid expansion of *colonias* (poorly planned and serviced housing estates) for the *maquila* workers (Frey 2003).

BOX 16 Underpolluted Regions and Indifference to Life

Lawrence Summers is president of Harvard University. Previously he was chief economist at the World Bank, then Undersecretary and (briefly) Secretary of the Treasury under US President Clinton. When he was at the World Bank, the media obtained a memo in which he defended, on cost-benefit grounds, the case for dumping toxic waste in countries where wages (and therefore the cost of illness) were lowest, and people most likely to die of something else first. The text of the memorandum (reproduced in Anton, Fisk & Holmstrom eds. 2000), the authenticity of which has never been questioned, follows:

DATE: December 12, 1991
TO: Distribution
FR: Lawrence H. Summers
Subject: GEP

"Dirty" Industries: Just between you and me, shouldn't the World Bank be encouraging MORE migration of the dirty industries to the LDCs? I can think of three reasons:

1) The measurement of the costs of health impairing pollution depends on the foregone earnings from increased morbidity and mortality. From this point of view a given amount of health impairing pollution should be done in the country with the lowest cost, which will be the country with the lowest wages. I think the economic logic behind dumping a load of toxic waste in the lowest wage country is impeccable and we should face up to that.

2) *The costs of pollution are likely to be non-linear as the initial increments of pollution probably have very low cost. I've always thought that under-populated countries in Africa are vastly UNDER-polluted, their air quality is probably vastly inefficiently low compared to Los Angeles or Mexico City. Only the lamentable facts that so much pollution is generated by non-tradable industries (transport, electrical generation) and that the unit transport costs of solid waste are so high prevent world welfare enhancing trade in air pollution and waste.*

3) *The demand for a clean environment for aesthetic and health reasons is likely to have very high income elasticity. The concern over an agent that causes a one in a million change in the odds of prostate cancer is obviously going to be much higher in a country where people survive to get prostate cancer than in a country where under 5 mortality is is 200 per thousand. Also, much of the concern over industrial atmosphere discharge is about visibility impairing particulates. These discharges may have very little direct health impact. Clearly trade in goods that embody aesthetic pollution concerns could be welfare enhancing. While production is mobile the consumption of pretty air is a non-tradable.*

The problem with the arguments against all of these proposals for more pollution in LDCs (intrinsic rights to certain goods, moral reasons, social concerns, lack of adequate markets, etc.) could be turned around and used more or less effectively against every Bank proposal for liberalization.

The final paragraph, often omitted when the document is reproduced, conclusively establishes a link with the broader market-driven economic logic of World Bank economic proposals. For the Bank (or at least for Summers), the protection from deadly environmental hazards you deserve is the protection you can pay for, and only that.

A final danger for Antonia involves the possibility that she might be tricked or kidnapped into the sex trade. Some 50,000 people annually are sexually trafficked into the USA by pimps and criminal gangs, a third of them from Latin America, and "[s]ex businesses are the largest sector of employment for women who have lost jobs as a result of globalization" (Ugarte, Zarate & Farley 2003:162). It is important not to exaggerate or sensationalize the sex trade, but it must be recognized as a real element of globalization and a growing problem worldwide (Hughes 2000, Richard 2000).

8 Globalization Comes Home to Roost

Our last vignette reminds us that globalization destroys lives even in high-income countries whose leaders have been among its most ardent proponents. Their simple aggregate wealth means that, other things being equal, high-income countries are better able to cope with the "shocks" of global market integration. At the same time, globalization is leading to a blurring of boundaries – evident, for example, in the spread to the US of such stereotypically "Third World" forms of work organization: as piecework automobile parts assembly by home-based workers (Gringeri 1994) and dangerous working conditions in meat packing plants that would not have been out of place a century ago (Human Rights Watch 2004). Walter Russell Mead (1992) warned that trade liberalization could result in a neo-Victorian world order in which "the First and Third worlds will not so much disappear as mingle. There will be more people in Mexico and India who live like Americans of the upper-middle class; on the other hand, there will be more – many more – people in the United States who live like the slum dwellers of Mexico City and Calcutta" (Mead 1992). This has not yet happened, but early warning signs in the USA and elsewhere – like Tom's precarious work situation[24] – are unmistakable. Several elements contribute to this trend.

Trade liberalization accelerates the loss of work and income for less qualified workers[25] in high-income (high-wage) countries, as those jobs shift to lower-wage nations (Dollar 2002). Simultaneously, the ability of corporate managers to relocate production (or to opt for a lower-cost supplier of outsourced activities) erodes the bargaining power of workers and their ability to negotiate better wages or protect their existing income and working conditions. Notably, full-time work in the industrialized countries has tended to be replaced by part-time, contract and temporary employment in the interests of lower costs and labour market 'flexibility'. *The Wall Street Journal* notes that: "Just as Japan perfected the just-in-time inventory system," which reduces costs by ensuring that parts arrive at the point of production literally minutes before being needed, "America is well on its way to perfecting the just-in-time work force, notwithstanding the grim toll it takes on labour. The harsh truth is that it is a major productivity plus" (Wysockij 1995).

These trends are most conspicuous in the USA, where labour markets are less regulated than anywhere else in the industrialized world. A review of recent changes in US income distribution concluded that "not only did workers on the bottom of the skill distribution fare poorly in terms of losing ground on wages, they also have less safe working conditions, found themselves working less regular shifts, had fewer benefits such as pensions and health care, and lower job security and job satisfaction" (Fligstein & Shin 2003).[26] Elsewhere, Germany is facing a policy dilemma as high technology firms threaten to move to lower-wage countries also blessed with a well-educated workforce, such as Hungary — leading German workers to accept longer working hours, lower pay and fewer benefits (Elliott 2004a). The spread of insecure or precarious work is not confined to "rust belt" manufacturing industries. The USA, for example, has experienced a loss of over 400,000 high-tech jobs since 2001, as firms outsource work to lower-wage countries that have improved the education levels of their workforces (Srivastava & Theodore 2004).

The rising number of personal bankruptcies in the United States is one of the consequences of the productivity gains from the "just-in-time workforce," and an especially disturbing indicator of the spread of work-related insecurity. There were 1.5 million filings in 2002 (Century Foundation 2004) and these numbers cannot tell us "how much more of the middle class is near the fragile edge of economic failure" (Sullivan, Warren & Westbrook 2000:74). In the most detailed study of household bankruptcies in the USA, 67.5 percent of respondents identified job-related reasons for filing (Sullivan, Warren and Westbrook 2004:16). On the other hand, incomes and entitlements are growing for those at the top of the economic pyramid (Wade 2002, Smeeding 2002), most notably in the United States but also in a number of other countries (WCSDG 2004:40-43), as illustrated by the growing gap between the pay of corporate CEOs and workers. In 1982 the ratio of average CEO salaries to average workers' pay in *Business Week's* top 365 corporations was 42/1. In 2003 it was 7 times greater, at 301/1 (Anderson et al. 2004).[27] "If the [US] minimum wage had increased as quickly as CEO pay has since 1990, it would today be $15.76 per hour, rather than the current $5.15 per hour" (Anderson et al. 2004:2).

At the low end of the income distribution, opportunities to contract out production or relocate it to low-wage jurisdiction have created worldwide wage competition. At the top end, managers and people with 'human capital' that can improve productivity and profitability can increasingly market themselves across national borders, which radically increases their bargaining power for much the same reason the bargaining power of workers is being eroded: "[Y]our real competitive position in the *world* economy is coming to depend on the function you perform in it" (Reich 1992:208, emphasis added). In addition, a "winner-take-all" effect (Frank & Cook 1995), makes it rational for employers to reward marginally better performance with much higher compensation. Few boards of directors can explain to their shareholders that they decided to pay a bit less for a second-best CEO or corporate law firm. Finally, the World Commission on the Social Dimensions of Globalization (2004:42) pointed to an increase in the share of national income going to capital as a contributor to rising inequality.

Meanwhile, social or 'welfare state' spending – at least since World War II, the mechanism by which industrialized societies have provided safety nets to guard against economic insecurity – has declined in high-income countries as a percentage of GDP over the 1980s and 1990s. Only four countries bucked this trend (Greece, Japan, Portugal and Turkey), and they were starting from a very low base. While the decline was slight in some countries (e.g. Switzerland, Iceland, Germany) it was dramatic in others: a drop of 28 percent in Ireland, 1986-1998; 21 percent in The Netherlands, 1983-98; and 19 percent in Canada, 1992-1999).[28] Some of the biggest spending declines occurred in areas most important to health: health care, cash transfers to (generally low-income) families, supports to unemployed workers and programs to increase labour market opportunities (OECD 2004a).

The decline in social spending partly results from revenue constraints created by tax competition among jurisdictions (Avi-Yonah 2000, Labonte et al. 2004:32-35). MNE managements can relocate both production and profits to jurisdictions where tax treatment is more favourable (see e.g. Weisman 2004) and wealthy households can similarly relocate their assets, and sometimes themselves. This decline can also be attributed to the much-neglected effect of globalization on the declining *political* power of organized labour — "the traditional coun-

terweight to the power of business" (WCSDG 2004:77) and historically the base of progressive social movements and social democratic
political parties. A large industrial working class still produces products for markets in North America and Western Europe. But unlike the
situation during the first three postwar decades, globalization means
that very large numbers of its members no longer live in these markets.
Instead they live and vote (or can't vote) in Mexico, Malaysia,
Indonesia, or China.

These points must be kept in mind when considering Smeeding's
conclusion that "[e]ven in a globalised world, the overall distribution of
income in a country remains very much a consequence of the domestic
political, institutional and economic choices made by those individual
countries" (Smeeding 2002:201). Certainly, there are marked differences among the G-20 countries[29]: the most unequal distributions of
income are found in Mexico, Russia, the USA, the UK and New
Zealand, while the most equal are in Sweden, Finland, Norway,
Denmark, Netherlands and Luxembourg. Canada, Taiwan and Central
European countries fall somewhere in the middle. Smeeding attributes
these differences to the stronger wage-setting institutions in the more
egalitarian countries, a result of higher rates of unionization and a cause
of better minimum wage standards, stronger collective bargaining
rights and more progressive forms of income redistribution and state-
supported welfare. Others (e.g. Esping-Anderson 1990, Coburn 2004)
organize high-income countries into three different categories: the
social democratic nations (such as the Scandinavian countries), in
which labour institutions and social policies remain strong; the corporatist states (such as Germany and France), in which social insurance
remains relatively generous and there is a strong emphasis on supporting families to provide essential welfare; and the liberal welfare state
(primarily the Anglo countries of the UK, the USA, Australia and New
Zealand), in which means-testing and market-based systems predomi-
nate. Not only income inequalities, but also disparities in key health
indicators such as infant mortality, increase along the continuum from
social democratic to liberal welfare states. In 1996, infant mortality
rates (IMR) in the *poorest* neighbourhoods in Canada, a country closer
to the corporatist than the liberal welfare states, were lower than the
average rate for all neighbourhoods in the USA; but IMRs in Canada's

richest neighbourhoods were higher than the average rate for all of Sweden (Coburn 2004).

What do these trends have to do with Tom, and with human health more generally?

A reasonably secure job that provides an adequate income is one of the axiomatic determinants of health. Not only does decent work provide individuals and families with the income to purchase the necessities for health; it is often where people form the friendships and social networks that independently and powerfully influence their health. It is a plus, of course, if the work is relatively healthy or safe – a desideratum that includes not only protection from accident hazards and chemical and biological pollutants, but also a work regime that does not exacerbate stress by combining high demands with low control over the pace and conditions of work (Karasek & Theorell 1990).

These conditions are now only a faint hope for millions of workers like Tom. "[F]ormerly well-paid, unionized...employees have been forced to seek employment in the expanding service sector, where full-time jobs are scarce, few employees have benefits or earn living wages, hours are irregular, and many employees hold down multiple jobs in an effort to survive" (Polanyi, Tompa & Foley 2004:70-71). One in five Canadian workers was employed part-time in 2003, one in four of them involuntarily – that is, s/he claimed to be looking for full-time work (Statistics Canada 2004). Counting temporary, self-employed and multiple (part-time) jobholders, like Tom, the number of Canadians in "non-standard" and more precarious employment rises to one in three (Polanyi, Tompa & Foley 2004).

Even as labour income is stagnant or declining for many workers their hours, workloads and work speed are rising rapidly, not only in Canada but also in almost all OECD countries. Workplace stress, work-related mental health problems and physical illness are rising in parallel, as is the number of workers experiencing difficulty in managing both work and family life (Duxbury & Higgins 2003, Higgins, Duxbury & Johnson 2004). In aging societies where social provision is being cut back, as in North America, increasing numbers of working people like

Tom will have to meet the competing demands of work and elder care as well. The multiple dimensions of work-related insecurity are important sources of stress: workers are not only unsure about their present employment and income and about prospects for the future, but also about the shrinking safety net of unemployment and welfare transfers (Quinlan, Mayhew & Bohle 2001, ILO 2004b, Polanyi, Tompa & Foley 2004). Canada's contribution to labour market flexibility has been a massive 60% decline in spending on supports for unemployed workers, as a percentage of GDP, between 1991 and 1999 (OECD 2004a). Cutbacks in the national unemployment insurance system were a major factor in the Canadian government's ability to balance its budget after years of running deficits, but they made it much harder for Tom, and others like him, to collect benefits after they lose a job and to survive on them – reducing the percentage of unemployed workers eligible for benefits to levels not seen since the original legislation of the 1940s (Rice & Prince 2000).

It is not a great leap from what the data tell us about the physical and mental health risks of part-time, insecure and precarious employment to Tom's accident. In Canada the risks are increased by the post-NAFTA integration of North American labour markets. Above and beyond the 'offshoring' of jobs, Canada has increasing difficulty in setting social and labour market policies independently of the US. Especially in central Canada, where Tom's accident occurred and where manufacturing industry is tightly linked to suppliers and customers in the US, the price tag of independence – measured in job losses, capital flight and foregone tax revenues – is high, and almost certainly rising. Canadian trends and policy responses therefore bear watching as early warning indicators of the challenges globalization will present for other high income countries.

9 Conclusion

The fundamental health challenges inherent in our contemporary global political economy – equity and sustainability — have been central to the struggle for health within countries for the past century. Addressing them requires some form of market-correcting system of wealth redistribution between, as well as within, nations. As Birdsall argues, globalization as we know it today is fundamentally asymmetric.

"In its benefits and its risks, it works less well for the currently poor countries and for poor households within developing countries. Because markets at the national level are asymmetric, modern capitalist economies have social contracts, progressive tax systems, and laws and regulations to manage asymmetries and market failures. At the global level, there is no real equivalent to national governments to manage global markets, though they are bigger, deeper and if anything more asymmetric. They work better for the rich; and their risks and failures hurt the poor more" (Birdsall 2002).

The national and global are linked. Globalization's present form limits the macroeconomic, development and health policy space within rich and poor nations alike. Liberalized capital markets "sanction deviations from orthodoxy" (WCSDG 2004:58), that is, anything that limits the potential for profit, and have "added to the speed at which, and the drama with which, financial markets bring retribution on governments whose policies are not 'credible' " (Glyn 1995:55). Liberalized trade still benefits high- more than low-income countries; and its rules-based system is frequently ignored or undermined by countries such as the US when the outcomes it generates are not in their own interests. The long-running dispute with Canada about softwood lumber is a case in point. Developing world debt is "perhaps the most efficient form of neocolonialism" (Bullard 2004). And the wealthy world's responses to disease crises sweeping many parts of the low-income world, while belatedly improving, are woefully inadequate and eclipsed by huge expenditures on attempts to make the world safer for high-income citizens through increased militarization and decreased civil rights (Oloka-Onyango & Udugama 2003).

Birdsall concludes that the discussion of whether globalization and openness is good or bad for the poor should move on to a discussion of "the appropriate global social contract and appropriate global arrangements for minimising the asymmetric risks and costs of global market failure". If we set aside scepticism about the assumption that "a civilizing hand" can rein in the more predatory elements of global capitalism, what should the contents of such a global social contract look like? In somewhat idealist tones, the World Commission on the Social Dimensions of Globalization urged a "rights-based" approach to globalization, in which the eradication of poverty and the attainment of the MDGs should be seen as the first steps towards a socioeconomic floor for the global economy, requiring in part "a more democratic governance of globalization" (WCSDG 2004). Its recommended reforms to move the global political economy in this direction resemble those that have been proffered at least for the past 20 years, as follows.

- Increases in untied development assistance to the long-standing, albeit non-binding UN target of 0.7% of rich countries' gross national income, along with efforts to mobilize additional sources of funding.

- Accelerated and deepened debt cancellation or relief relative to levels available under the enhanced HIPC initiative – although the report does not specifically recommend debt cancellation for countries not eligible under enhanced HIPC.

- Trade agreements that substantially reduce unfair barriers to market access, especially for goods in which developing countries have a strong comparative advantage such as agricultural products.

- Stepped up actions to ensure core human and labour rights for workers around the world, with particular emphasis on gender inequalities.

- A multilateral framework to manage the international flow of people, such as the 'brain drain' of education professionals from poor to rich countries and its frequent corollary of 'brain waste' after they migrate.

- Stronger voting rights for low- and middle-income countries at the World Bank and IMF.

- Building on existing frameworks for international tax cooperation as a vital element in strengthening the integrity of national tax systems in all countries, increasing public resources for development and facilitating the fight against tax havens, money laundering and the financing of terrorism.

- Increased coherence in the global economic, financial and health/human rights system, and heads of state to promote policies in international fora that focus on well-being and quality of life.

In at least two areas – the relation of trade agreements to human rights obligations and the internationalization of taxation and wealth redistribution – a need exists for policy initiatives that go further than the commission's recommendations.

On the first point, the UN special rapporteurs on globalization and human rights have said it is necessary "to move away from approaches that are ad hoc and contingent" in ensuring that human rights, including the right to health, are not compromised by trade liberalization (Oloka-Onyango & Udugama 2003). The initial report from the UN's special rapporteur on the right of everyone to the highest attainable standard of physical and mental health (as specified in the International Covenant on Economic, Social and Cultural Rights) outlined an expansive interpretation of the right, which explicitly included poverty-related issues (Hunt 2003). His subsequent examination of the WTO regime led to the conclusion that "the form, pacing and sequencing of trade liberalization [must] be conducive to the progressive realization of the right to health" and that "progressive realization of the right to health, and the immediate obligations to which it is subject, place reasonable conditions on the trade rules and policies that may be chosen" (Hunt 2004:24). High priority should be given to ensuring that both the content of trade agreements and the operations of the WTO (including its dispute settlement mechanism, which was not considered in the 2004 report) and other trade policy institutions conform to this principle.

On the second point, recognition is growing of both the desirability and the difficulty of devising some mechanism of global income transfers. Yunker (2004) uses a global econometric model (the World

Economic Equalization Programme, or WEEP) to simulate the effects over a 50-year period of a "global Marshall Plan" to raise economic growth in the developing world using major increases in development assistance financed by national treasuries. While he is candid about the huge uncertainties inherent in such simulations, he concludes that if such a programme were implemented, "the living standards of what are the poorest countries of today would have improved sufficiently, by the end of the period, to be comparable to those of the richest countries today." This result, inconceivable in a business-as-usual scenario, is relatively insensitive to variations in key assumptions. However, it would require annual development assistance commitments by the rich countries on the order of 2-4% of GNI or GNP – far higher than the 0.7% target, now reached by only a few countries (Figure 4). It is not clear why Yunker regards the costs of such a capital transfer as within the realm of political acceptability.

If such national commitments are unlikely, what international revenue-raising mechanisms might be considered? Taxing holdings in off-shore accounts is one option. According to the IMF, about $8 trillion is held in such accounts. Assuming a 5 percent return, taxed at 40 percent, this would raise $160 billion a year (UNRISD 2000:xi) – about the estimated amount of extra financing needed to reach the Millennium Development Goals (UN Millennium Project 2005). Numerous other options have been proposed, notably by a group of experts convened by France's President Chirac (Groupe de travail 2004). These include taxes on arms sales, shipping, international air travel or jet fuel, and carbon emissions (Clunies-Ross 2004, Groupe de travail 2004). A currency transaction tax of 0.25%, the so-called Tobin tax after the economist who first proposed it, would generate over $170 billion annually, according to one estimate, although other policy measures suggest that revenues would be considerably less, and is technically feasible (Arestis & Sawyer 1999, Clunies-Ross 2004). Other suggestions include a general tax on securities transactions and a surcharge on corporate income taxes paid by large corporations; a much higher degree of multilateral consensus exists on the need to curb evasion of existing taxes levied at the national level (Groupe de travail 2004).

Even more than others we have described, international taxation confronts formidable political difficulties. Although some such taxes could actually improve economic efficiency, for instance by reducing the creation of negative externalities in the form of uncompensated environmental damage (Groupe de travail 2004), they would represent challenges to present global distributions of wealth and power.

BOX 17 Global Corporate Social Responsibility

Attempts to create UN mandatory codes of conduct for multinational enterprises (MNEs) in the 1970s were abandoned in the 1980s, with the rise of Reagan and Thatcher in the USA and the UK, respectively. Recommendations for supranational environmental regulation of MNEs drafted for the first World Summit on Sustainable Development (the Rio Summit of 1992) were similarly dropped after pressure from corporations (Richter 2001). In place of compulsory codes came a crowd of voluntary or self-regulatory initiatives, such as the Social Accountability International auditing project of the USA, the Ethical Trading Initiative in the UK, the OECD's Guidelines on MNEs and, most recently, the United Nations' Global Compact. All of these encourage MNE compliance with core social, labour and environmental standards embodied in different human rights covenants and treaties, or UN declarations (Barrientos & Kabeer 2004, Murray 2004).

Proponents of voluntary codes claim that, in contrast to government regulations, they are cheaper, allow for corporate innovation and are more flexible in adapting to dynamic labour and social conditions in diverse countries (Murray 2004). Ironically, these proponents are often the same ones arguing the necessity of an enforceable rules-based global trading system. The growth in religious group and NGO monitoring of MNEs, and subsequent media publicity, is also claimed to be a form of global check on the limitations of corporate self-regulation and self-disclosure. Sceptics contend that voluntary codes contain few, if any, enforcement measures, lack clarity or specificity, omit such key rights as free association or the right to strike, rely upon ongoing civil society scrutiny, do not ensure corporate transparency and so far have no shown no evidence of working (Richter 2001, Murray 2004). Indeed, a study of workplace democracy in the USA concluded that companies voluntarily adopting progressive labour policies stood to lose ground to those that did not, particularly a production became more globalized (Levine 1995). Its conclusion: Only a regulatory requirement creating a 'level playing field' for all competitors would sustain efforts to create healthier, more democratic workplaces. Similarly, an unofficial Commission on Canadian Democracy and Corporate Accountability concluded in 2002 that "voluntary CSR [corporate social responsibility], at its best, supplements legal regulation by aiming for standards higher than those existing in law. It is not a replacement..." (Canadian Democracy and Corporate Accountability Commission 2002:13, our emphasis).

A key, and unresolved, question is that of the political viability of regulation that substantially increases costs while national and sub-national jurisdictions compete for hypermobile investment capital; and when most consumers seem more concerned with quality and price rather than with the conditions under which the goods and services they buy are produced and delivered. An intuitively attractive solution is the development of multilaterally agreed upon standards for corporate conduct. Although a detailed assessment of the prospects for such standards is far outside the scope of this chapter, the example of efforts to control bribery and other forms of corruption involving public officials (see Box 8) demonstrates both their potential effectiveness and their reliance on political commitment and forensic creativity at the national (and sometimes sub-national) level.

Afterword

At a few points in this book, we have made reference to the G8 countries. This book itself has its origins in an earlier project that produced a 'report card' on the health implications of commitments made at the 1999-2001 G8 Summit meetings (Labonte et al. 2004, Labonte and Schrecker 2004). Our presumption was (and is) that these countries, accounting for roughly half the world's economic activity and with just under half the votes in the decision-making of the World Bank and the International Monetary Fund, bear special responsibility for the international community's success or failure in meeting such objectives as the Millennium Development Goals (Box 10), most of which are either directly or indirectly related to health. As Figure 4 shows, at least if ODA is an appropriate measure of commitment, the G7 (the G8 countries minus Russia, which is now in no position to provide development assistance) have actually lagged behind some other countries in this respect. Our work, in fact, demonstrated a pattern in which commitments were either (a) only partly fulfilled, or (b) fulfilled, yet demonstrably not commensurate with the scale of unmet needs.

The book goes to press in the months leading up to the 2005 Summit in the United Kingdom. Among the G8, France and the UK have taken the lead in a number of areas (HM Treasury & DFID 2003, Groupe de travail 2004), and the wide publicity given to the conclusions of the UN Millennium Project (2005) has given rise to cautious optimism about the prospects for a meaningful response to the challenge presented by the MDGs. Critical action items include the triad of increased aid, debt cancellation and fairer trade (Labonte, Schrecker, in press), as well as such urgent issues as increased investment in research on diseases of the poor (Global Forum for Health Research 2004). On the other hand, the arguments we have made here suggest that meeting the challenge may require not just incremental increases to existing commitments, but fundamental challenges to the priorities and values that guide political and economic decision-making on an international scale. History suggests that such changes demand radical (and not always non-violent) forms of political mobilization and action. Although history has not yet encountered such a demand on a global scale, it is worth recalling that the political difficulties of abolishing slavery and implementing maximum hours of work were also once thought to be insurmountable.

Endnotes

1 Reported in Kahn & Yardley (2004)

2 For a more cautious and nuanced evaluation of the Ugandan experience, which emphasizes the overall constraints created by poverty, see O'Manique (2004: 135-268)

3 Mercantilism refers to 18th century European capitalism in which the state regulated the sale and purchase of goods to maximize national economic growth by favouring producers within its own borders (and its own colonies).

4 The lead British negotiator at the post-World War Two Bretton Woods conference that created the IMF and World Bank, John Maynard Keynes, initially proposed a global bank, the 'International Clearing Union,' which would fix exchange rates between nations and, through an intricate scheme of incentives and penalties, pressure countries to avoid a trade deficit or trade surplus, both of which are destabilizing and liable to worsen global economic inequalities. His proposition, though supported by Europe, Latin America and the Commonwealth, was rejected by the USA (Monbiot 2003).

5 All amounts in this Chapter are in US$.

6 FDI experienced a continuous rise over the 1990s, much of it going into mergers and acquisitions, rather than into 'green field' investment — that is, the building of new establishments (UNCTAD 2004a). This led to a sharp decline in 2001-2003, as multinational enterprises were forced to sell off some of their assets to pay for their precipitous buying spree. FDI also brings with it costs to developing countries to reduce the risk of currency inflation if too much investment is received too rapidly. Many developing countries have further liberalized their economies and altered their domestic policies, for instance by extending 'tax holidays,' to attract FDI (UNCTAD, 2004a). In summary, even FDI, in contrast to portfolio or speculative investment, is not an automatic route to 'healthy' economic growth; and contrary to much conventional rhetoric about its value to 'jump start' growth in poorer countries, FDI tends to *follow* growth rather than to lead it (Labonte et al. 2004:30-31).

7   http://www.un.org/Overview/rights.html

8   Even if they win a WTO dispute, low-income countries are unlikely to use trade-sanctions to 'punish' the offending high-income country. The USA, for example, recently lost a WTO case concerning Internet gambling to the small Caribbean nation of Antigua and Barbuda. The USA will appeal the decision, potentially adding years to its eventual resolution, and has indicated that, even if the appeal loses, it will retain its policy on Internet gambling since there are no effective remedies the small island nations can implement (*Bridges* 2004d).

We leave aside a more detailed critique of how WTO negotiations, while nominally democratic, are biased structurally in favour of high-income countries through, as examples, high-income countries' much larger negotiating teams, control over special 'green room' meetings or pre-ministerial gatherings to help shape and manage the ministerial negotiations, the pro-liberalization (rather than neutral) stance of the WTO's 550 staff, 80 per cent of whom come from high-income countries (see Jawara & Kwa 2003). Even Dollar, a liberalization proponent, argues that the dispute settlement structure of the WTO is inherently unbalanced with all of the advantage going to high-income countries with their asymmetrically large economies (Dollar 2002), which has led some WTO reformers to urge the use of GNI-weighted fines rather than trade sanctions as penalties.

We also leave aside discussion of similarities and differences between the WTO and the European Union (EU), another supranational organization with even more extensive constraints on national governments. The EU, however, is a *political* union that incorporates elected legislative representation (in the European Parliament) as well as multiple executive-level structures of consultation and coordination, and (in the case of the Schengen countries) largely unrestricted migration across national borders. At the same time, EU policies are still potentially subordinated to the provisions of WTO agreements.

9   The G8 (Group of 8) countries are Canada, France, Germany, Italy, Japan, Russia the USA and the UK, with special membership sta-

tus given to the European Union. Russia was only accepted as a full member of what was previously the G7 in 2003, and does not yet participate in meetings of the G7 finance ministers.

[10] The figure often cited is an average 9 percent annual growth in GDP/per capita over the 1990s, based on official government data. Others argue that this is an inflated figure and the truer rate of annual growth is between 5 – 6 percent (Wade 2002:48).

[11] Deaton (2004b), amongst others, shows a relatively weak relationship between economic growth, poverty reduction and changes in life expectancy in poorer countries over the last half-century. He shows that the transfer ('globalization') of health knowledge and technologies such as vaccines, antibiotics, sanitation, oral rehydration therapy and infectious disease vector controls likely played the major part in shrinking the health gap between the world's rich and poor. However, he also acknowledges that some degree of growth and poverty reduction is essential to sustain these improvements into the future and that, while some countries were able to improve childhood mortality "even in the absence of economic growth ... gains in income were undoubtedly important for improving nutrition, and for funding for better water and sanitation schemes" (p.29). Moreover, the 'gradient effect' found in high-income countries, in which health status by almost any measure worsens as one goes down the hierarchy of income or social class, and is worst for the poorest, underscores the public health pre-eminence given to poverty – whether defined in absolute or relative terms – as one of the most fundamental determinants of health.

[12] Earlier findings, primarily from the USA, found that states with higher income inequalities had poorer overall health status (i.e. higher standardized mortality rates). These findings have since been challenged on methodological and empirical grounds, as income data sets on a larger number of countries have become available. Much of the income inequality effects on health in the USA disappear when other inequality stratifiers, such as race and education, are controlled for. Coburn (2004:43), in an important commentary on this debate, points out "income inequality may be correlated with health but...probably reflects or is a proxy for a variety of social conditions, operating through individual and col-

lective, material and psycho-social pathways, rather than...being a single main cause of poorer health." As one example of a social condition: Access to publicly funded universal health care is generally not counted as income in health inequalities research. A study of one Canadian province, however, found that when a monetary value was assigned to the benefits of health services provided by our tax-funded universal health care system, the effect was to reduce the post-tax/transfer income difference between the richest and poorest population deciles by a substantial 20 per cent (Mustard et al. 1998).

13 Dollar (2002:25), however, also acknowledges that this supposed equalizing trend will nonetheless crest around 2015, after which global income inequalities will again rise rapidly.

14 Income inequalities existed before contemporary globalization. Brazil's inequalities, for example, are a legacy of colonialism, but they worsened considerably from 1960 through the mid 1990s before beginning a slow reversal due to policies aimed at improving the labour income of the poorest quintile (Clements 1997). Nor can, or should, the geography of globalization's contemporary winners and losers be ignored. Low- and middle-income countries that have gained most from global market integration are ones with easier access to trading routes, mostly ocean shipping. Landlocked countries, or regions within individual nations, have done less well, particularly when, as with most countries in sub-Saharan Africa, they also lack a good domestic transportation infrastructure because imperial powers had little reason to make the necessary investments.

15 *Maquiladoras,* the Mexican term for EPZs, for example, account for 50 per cent of that country's exports (Schwartz 2002).

16 Second-hand clothing is officially subject to a 25 percent import duty applied to all clothing entering Zambia. But because the clothing has no stated value in the country from which it comes, no duty is charged on it (Mtonga & Chikoti 2002). Zambia was also unable to export its clothing, since many other African countries had also opened their markets to second-hand products; while new clothing imports were generally manufactured with cotton that was

heavily subsidized by high-income country producers, particularly in the USA.

17 Former Zambian president Kenneth Kaunda stated that for many years his country refused to borrow from the IMF. But when world copper prices plummeted just as world oil prices soared, "We had no choice. I approached the IMF and the World Bank and said: Look, we are in this precarious situation. Can we borrow? Their reply was, well, we think that copper prices will soon rise again, so please feel free to borrow" (quoted in Jeter 2002). Copper prices, however, continued to plunge, and Zambia's debt began to grow.

18 Debt cancellation costs are routinely included as part of a donor country's ODA budget. Thus, the $825 million that African countries owe to Export Development Canada (an export credit agency) and the Canadian Wheat Board (a marketing agency that guarantees minimum producer prices for wheat exports) will, as these debts are cancelled over the next few years, be reckoned as almost 20 per cent of Canada's staged increase in development assistance for African countries (Canadian Council for International Cooperation Africa-Canada Forum 2002).

19 That is, the value of the debt (principal and interest) in today's dollars, after discounting for future inflation to reflect the fact that it need only be repaid in the future.

20 The IMF, for example, requires Zambia to restrict its government payroll bill to 8% of GDP. But to prevent professionals from leaving the country, and to retain desperately needed teachers and health workers, wage packets and supports have caused the payroll bill to climb to 9% of GDP. Zambia was suspended from debt-relief in 2004, and must pay $300 million in annual debt servicing costs as a result. Moreover, to get back on debt-relief, Zambia must privatize its remaining energy and communication sectors, and use the proceeds of the sales – not for health or education – but to pay down its debts. (See: "Life Under the IMF's Magnifying Glass," Bretton Woods Update No. 39. March -April 2004. http://www.brettonwoodsproject.org/update/39/index.shtml.)

21 As one example, all US food aid, and about 90 percent of Canadian food aid, comes from American or Canadian producers. This helps

food producers in these countries during counter-cyclical periods (supply exceeding demand) but can severely damage the domestic markets for food producers within aid-receiving countries. For this reason most other donor countries provide food aid in the form of grants, with which recipient countries can purchase what foods they require (which may not always include wheat or corn!), as they require it, and in ways that do not damage markets for their own growers.

22 High-income countries also mine each other for skilled labour, creating a global hierarchy of recruitment. With respect to physicians, some 8000 Canadian-trained doctors now practice in the USA; 25 per cent of practising physicians in Canada (mostly in rural areas) are foreign-trained, many from South Africa; and almost 80 per cent of rural South African physicians are from other countries, notably Cuba and other SSA nations (Martineau et al. 2004).

23 Both Dollar (2002) and Wade (2002) point out that unskilled labour is presently in oversupply in low-income countries. Not only would increased migration of unskilled labour to high-income countries raise the remittances of foreign currency to low-income nations; it would also improve labour's negotiating power in such countries, slowly improving wages, health and living/working conditions.

24 In 2001, corn cost $3.41 a barrel to produce in the USA, but sold on the world market for $2.28, the direct result of US government subsidies to its corn producers (Carlsen 2003).

25 Article XX(b) of GATT permits exception to WTO rules "necessary to protect human, animal or plant life or health." Part of the reason why only one case has so far been successful is that countries wishing to derogate from trade rules under this exception are responsible for proving that the measure is not really protectionism in disguise. Many health non-governmental organizations (NGOs) argue that a reverse onus should apply, i.e., the complaining country should prove that the exception was not invoked to protect human, animal or plant life or health.

26 Health insurance is covered in the GATS section dealing with financial services, and so has sometimes been overlooked by trade negotiators. Even Canada, which has stated that it will not make

any commitments to liberalize health care under GATS, agreed in 1994 to liberalize trade in health insurance services. This means that, should Canada extend its public health insurance monopoly for physician and hospital services into areas in which there are currently private health insurance providers (e.g. for dental care, pharmaceuticals or home care), a trade challenge could result (Sanger & Sinclair 2004).

27 For a very similar real world example (not a composite), see Witte (2004).

28 We use "less qualified" in preference to the more familiar "low-skilled," because many professors and journalists in the industrialized world could not do the work (cf. Ehrenreich 2000).

29 For more detailed information on this pattern, see the State of Working America reports produced by the Economic Policy Institute (www.epinet.org), most recently Mishel, Bernstein and Allegretto (2004).

30 Particularly disturbing is the fact that CEOs of firms that outsource the largest number of jobs to low-wage offshore locations, and that make the most aggressive use of foreign subsidiaries for tax avoidance, consistently get bigger raises that the average (Anderson et al. 2003, 2004).

31 Comparisons are for the year of highest social spending post-1980 to the most recent year of data. Source: OECD (2004a).

32 The G-20 is an informal forum of 20 industrial and some middle income emerging-market countries created in 1999 to meet a perceived need for closer cooperation on key issues related to the international monetary and financial system.

References

Abbasi K. Changing sides. *British Medical Journal*, 1999, 318:865-1208.

Adams P. Submission to the U.S. Senate Committee on Foreign Relations Regarding the MDB Roundtable Discussion on Multilateral Development Bank Corruption October 29, 2004. New York, Probe International Foundation, 2004 (http://www.odiousdebts.org/odious-debts/publications/SenateWrittenSubmissionFinal.pdf, accessed 1 February 2005).

Adlung R, Carzaniga A. Health services under the General Agreement on Trade in Services. In: Vieira C, Drager N, eds. *Trade in health services: global, regional and country perspectives*. Washington, DC, Pan American Health Organization, 2002:13-33.

Albelda R, Withorn A, eds. Reforming welfare, redefining poverty. *Annals of the American Academy of Political and Social Science*, 577, 2001.

AFL-CIO. Section 301 Petition [to Office of the United States Trade Representative] of American Federation of Labor and Congress of Industrial Organizations. Washington, DC, AFL-CIO, 2004. (http://www.aflcio.org/issuespolitics/globaleconomy/upload/china_petition.pdf, accessed 1 February 2005).

Akin JS, Dow WH, Lance PM. Did the distribution of health insurance in China continue to grow less equitable in the nineties? Results from a longitudinal survey. *Social Science & Medicine*, 2004, 58:293-304.

Anderson S, Cavanagh J. Corporate empires. *Multinational Monitor*, 1996, 17(12) (http://multinationalmonitor.org/hyper/mm1296.08.html, accessed 1 February 2005).

Anderson S, Cavanagh J. Of the world's 100 largest economic entities, 51 are now corporations and 49 are countries. Washington, DC, The Institute for Policy Studies, 2000 (http://www.corporations.org/system/top100.html, accessed 1 February 2005).

Anderson S, et al. Executive excess 2003 CEOs win, workers and tax-payers lose. Boston, Institute for Policy Studies, United for a Fair Economy, 2003. (http://www.faireconomy.org/press/2003/EE2003.pdf, accessed 1 February 2005).

Anderson S, et al. Executive excess 2004: campaign contributions, outsourcing, unexpensed stock options and rising CEO pay. Boston, Institute for Policy Studies, United for a Fair Economy, 2004 (http://www.faireconomy.org/press/2004/EE2004.pdf, accessed 1 February 2005).

Anonymous. America's new utopias. *The Economist*, 2001, August 30 (http://www.economist.com/printedition/displayStory.cfm?Story_ID=7 60545, accessed 1 February 2005).

Anonymous. Mexico's economy: the sucking sound from the East. *The Economist*, 2003, 26 July:35-36.

Anton A, Fisk M, Holmstrom N, eds. *Not for sale: in defense of public goods.* Boulder, Westview, 2000.

Arestis P, Sawyer M. What role for the Tobin tax in world economic governance? In: Michie M, Smith JG, eds. *Global instability: the political economy of world economic governance.* London, Routledge, 1999:151-167.

Armada F, Muntaner C, Navarro V. Health and social security reforms in Latin America: the convergence of the World Health Organization, the World Bank, and transnational corporations. *International Journal of Health Services*, 2001, 31(4):729-768.

Athreya B. *Trade is a women's issue.* New York, Global Policy Forum, 2003 (http://www.globalpolicy.org/socecon/inequal/labor/2003/0220women. htm, accessed 1 February 2005).

Atkinson S, et al. The referral process and urban health care in sub-Saharan Africa: the case of Lusaka, Zambia. *Social Science & Medicine*, 1999, 49:27-38.

Attac-Quebec, Tax Justice Network. Income tax reductions: the myth of job creation and economic growth. Paper is from a joint workshop of Attac-Quebec and the Tax Justice Network held at the World Social Forum IV, January 20, 2004 in Mumbai, India 2004 (http://www.taxjustice.net/all/pdf/incometaxreduction.pdf, accessed 1 February 2005).

Avi-Yonah R. Globalization, tax competition, and the fiscal crisis of the welfare state. *Harvard Law Review*, 2000, 113:1573-1676.

Barraza-Llorens M, et al. Addressing inequity in health and health care in Mexico. *Health Affairs*, 2002, 21:47-56.

Barrientos S, Kabeer N. Enhancing female employment in global production. *Global Social Policy*, 2004, 4(2):153-169.

Bartlett B. A tax increase is in the forecast. Dallas and Washington, DC, National Centre for Policy Analysis, 2004 (http://www.ncpa.org/edo/bb/2004/20041201bb.htm, accessed 1 February 2005).

Basu S. AIDS, empire, and public health behaviourism. *Equinet Newsletter*, 2003, 28. (http://www.equinetafrica.org/newsletter/index.php?issue=28, accessed 1 February 2005).

Bauman Z. *Globalization: the human consequences.* Cambridge, Polity Press, 1998.

Birdsall N. A stormy day on an open field: asymmetry and convergence in the global economy. In: Gruen D, O'Brien T, Lawson J, eds. *Globalisation, living standards and inequality: recent progress and continuing challenges,* proceedings of a conference held in Sydney, 27-28 May 2002. Canberra, Reserve Bank of Australia, Canberra, 2002:37-65 (http://www.rba.gov.au/PublicationsAndResearch/Conferences/2002/, accessed 1 February 2005).

Bisset R, Flint D, Kirkpatrick C, Mitlin D & Westlake K. Sustainability Impact Assessment of Proposed WTO Negotiations, Environmental Services. University of Manchester/Institute for Development Policy and Management, 2003. (http://idpm.man.ac.uk/sia-trade, accessed 9 November 2003).

Bloom DE, Canning D. The Health and Poverty of Nations: from theory to practice. *Journal of Human Development*, 2003, 4(1):47-71.

Bloom DE, Williamson JG. Demographic transitions and economic miracles in emerging Asia. *The World Bank Economic Review*, 1998, 12(3): 419-455.

Blustein P. U.S. wants to cancel poorest nations' debt. *The Washington Post*, 14 September 2004, A:06.

Bond P. *Against global apartheid: South Africa meets the World Bank, IMF and international finance.* Cape Town, University of Cape Town Press, 2001.

Bonnel R. Economic analysis of HIV/AIDS. Washington, DC, World Bank, AIDS campaign team for Africa, 2000 (ADF 2000 background paper). (http://www.iaen.org/files.cgi/435_HIVEconAnalysisADF.pdf, accessed 1 February 2005).

Bosshard P, et al. Gambling with people's lives: what the World Bank's new "high-risk/high-reward" strategy means for the poor and the environment. Washington, DC, Environmental Defense, Friends of the Earth, International Rivers Network, Washington, DC, 2003.

Bourguignon F. The poverty-growth-inequality triangle, paper presented at the Indian Council for Research on International Economic Relations, New Delhi, February 4, 2004. Washington, DC, World Bank, 2004 (http://econ.worldbank.org/files/33634_PovertyInequalityGrowthTrian gleFeb24.pdf, accessed 1 February 2005).

Bradshaw D, et al. Initial burden of disease estimates for South Africa 2000. *South African Medical Journal*, 2003, 93:682-688.

Bridges Weekly Trade News Digest 6[34]. 2002a (http://www.ictsd.org/weekly/index.htm, accessed 1 February 2005).

Bridges Weekly Trade News Digest 6[40]. 2002b (http://www.ictsd.org/weekly/index.htm, accessed 1 February 2005).

Bridges Weekly Trade News Digest 8[11]. 2004a (http://www.ictsd.org/weekly/index.htm, accessed 1 February 2005).

Bridges Weekly Trade News Digest 8[27]. 2004b
(http://www.ictsd.org/weekly/index.htm, accessed 1 February 2005).

Bridges Weekly Trade News Digest 8[38]. 2004c
(http://www.ictsd.org/weekly/index.htm, accessed 1 February 2005).

Bridges Weekly Trade News Digest 8[40]. 2004d
(http://www.ictsd.org/weekly/index.htm, accessed 1 February 2005).

Brock K, McGee R. *Mapping trade policy: understanding the challenges of civil society participation,* Working paper 225. Brighton, Sussex, Institute for Development Studies, 2004
(http://www.ids.ac.uk/ids/bookshop/wp/wp225.pdf, accessed 1 February 2005).

Budds J, McGranahan G. Are the debates on water privatization missing the point? Experiences from Africa, Asia and Latin America. *Environment & Urbanization*, 2003, 15: 87-114.

Bullard N. The new elite consensus? *Global Social Policy*, 2004, 4(2):143-152.

Cameron D, Stein JG . *Globalization triumphant or globalization in retreat: implications for Canada.* Ottawa, Department of Justice, Canada Research and Statistics Division, 2000 (rp02-6e) (http://canada.justice.gc.ca/en/ps/rs/rep/RP2002-6.pdf, accessed 1 February 2005).

Cammack P. What the World Bank means by povery reduction and why it matters. *New Political Economy*, 2004, 9(2):189-211.

Campbell C. Migrancy, masculine identities and AIDS: The psychosocial context of HIV transmission on the South African gold mines. *Social Science and Medicine*, 1997, 45:273-282.

Campbell D. Havens that have become a tax on the world's poor. *The Guardian*, 21 September 2004.

Canadian Council for International Cooperation Africa-Canada Forum. *Canadian economic relations with sub-Saharan Africa: recent trends.* Ottawa, Canadian Council for International Cooperation, 2002 (http://www.ccic.ca/e/docs/003_acf_revised_sept_can_economic_relation_africa.pdf, accessed 1 February 2005).

Canadian Democracy and Corporate Accountability Commission. *The new balance sheet. Corporate profits and responsibility in the 21st century*, Toronto, Thistle Printing, 2002 (http://www.atkinsonfoundation.ca/publications/FullReport2002.pdf, accessed 21 February 2005).

Carlsen L. The Mexican farmers' movement: exposing the myths of free trade. Silver City, New Mexico, Americas Program, Interhemispheric Resource Center, 2003. (http://www.americaspolicy.org/pdf/reports/0302farm.pdf, accessed 1 February 2005).

Cash RA, Narasimhan V. Impediments to global surveillance of infectious disease: economic and social consequences of open reporting. *Development*, 1999, 42(4):115-120.

Centre for Public Integrity. *Promoting Privatization*, 2003. (http://www.icij.org/dtaweb/water, accessed 28 February, 2003).

Century Foundation. *Life and debt: why American families are borrowing to the hilt.* New York, 2004 (http://www.tcf.org/Publications/EconomicsInequality/baker_debt.pdf, accessed 1 February 2005).

Chan A. Globalization, China's free (read bonded) labor market and the Chinese Trade Union. *Asia Pacific Business Review*, 2000, 6(3-4):260-281.

Chan A. A "race to the bottom": globalisation and China's labour standards. *China Perspectives*, 2003, March-April(46):41-49.

Chang HJ. *Kicking away the ladder: development strategy in historical perspective,* London, Anthem Press, 2002.

Charnovitz S. The supervision of health and biosafety regulation by world trade rules. *Tulane Environmental Law Journal*, 2000, 13(2).

Chen L, Berlinguer G. Health equity in a globalizing world. In: Whitehead M, et al., eds. *Challenging inequities in health: from ethics to action*. New York, Oxford University Press, 2001:34-44.

Chen L, Evans T, Anand S, Boufford J, Brown H, Chowdhury M et al. Human resources for health: overcoming the crisis. *The Lancet,* 2004, 364:1984-1990.

Chen S, Ravallion M. How have the world's poorest fared since the early 1980s? Washington, DC Development Research Group, World Bank, 2004. (http://papers.ssrn.com/sol3/papers.cfm?abstract_id=610385, accessed 1 February 2005).

Chen S, Wang Y. China's growth and poverty reduction: recent trends between 1990 and 1999. Washington, DC: World Bank, 2001 (http://econ.worldbank.org/files/2369_wps2651.pdf, accessed 1 February 2005).

China Daily. Big FDI inflows pose no threat. *China Daily*, 28 April 2004 (http://www.china.org.cn/english/international/94243.htm, accessed 1 February 2005).

Chirac J. President of France Jacques Chirac's Address to the U.N. General Assembly. *The New York Times*, 23 September 2003.

Citizens for Tax Justice. Year-by-year analysis of the Bush tax cuts shows growing tilt to the very rich, Washington, DC, 2002 (http://www.ctj.org/pdf/gwb0602.pdf, accessed 21 February 2005).

Citizens for Tax Justice. Details on the Bush tax cuts so far (as of fall 2003). Washington, DC, 2003 (http://www.ctj.org/pdf/gwbdata.pdf, accessed 15 January 2005).

Clements B. Income distribution and social expenditures in Brazil. Washington, DC, International Monetary Fund, 1997 (IMF Working Paper WP/97/120) (http://www.imf.org/external/pubs/ft/wp/wp97120.pdf, accessed 1 February 2005).

Clunies-Ross A. Resources for social development. *Global Social Policy*, 2004, 4(2):197-214.

Cobham A. Capital Account Liberalization and Poverty. *Global Social Policy*, 2002, 2(2):163-188.

Coburn D. Beyond the income inequality hypothesis: class,neo-liberalism, and health inequalities. *Social Science and Medicine*, 2004, 58:41-56.

Collins J, Lear J. *Chile's free-market miracle: a second look.* Oakland, CA, Food First Books, 1995.

Commission on Macroeconomics and Health. *Macroeconomics and health: investing in health for economic development.* Geneva, World Health Organization, 2001 (http://www.cid.harvard.edu/cidcmh/CMHReport.pdf, accessed 21 February 2005).

Condesa Consulting Group. Mexico Agricultural Situation: Summary of Mexican government study on the effects of NAFTA on Mexican agriculture, USDA Foreign Agricultural Service Report MX4070. Washington, DC, Global Agriculture Information Network, 2004 (http:/www.sice.oas.org/geograph/westernh/naftamexagri_e.pdf, accessed 1 February 2005).

Connolly CP. The role of private security in combatting terrorism. *Journal of Homeland Security*, 2003 (http://www.homelandsecurity.org/journal/Commentary/Connolly.html, accessed 1 February 2005).

Cornia GA, Addison T, Kiiski S. Income distribution changes and their impact in the post-Second World War period. In: Cornia GA, ed., *Inequality, growth, and poverty in an era of liberalization and globalization,* UNU-WIDER Studies in Development Economics. Oxford, Oxford University Press, 2004: 26-54.

Cornia GA, Jolly R, Stewart F, eds. *Adjustment with a human face, vol. 1: protecting the vulnerable and promoting growth.* Oxford, Clarendon Press, 1987.

Das BL. *The World Trade Organization: A Guide to New Frameworks for International Trade.* London, Zed Books, 2000.

De Paula L, Alves Jr A. External financial fragility and the 1998-99 Brazilian currency crisis. *Journal of Post Keynesian Economics*, 2000, 22(4):589-617.

Deaton A. Health, inequality, and economic development. Geneva, World Health Organization Commission on Macroeconomics and Health, 2001 (CMH working paper series WG1:3: http://www.cmhealth.org/docs/wg1_paper3.pdf, accessed 1 February 2005).

Deaton A. Measuring poverty in a growing world (or measuring gowth in a poor world). Princeton, Research Program in Development Studies, Woodrow Wilson School, Princeton University, February 2004a;
(http://www.wws.princeton.edu/%7Erpds/downloads/deaton_measuringpoverty_204.pdf, accessed 1 February 2005)

Deaton A. Health in an age of globalization, Princeton, Research Program in Development Studies, Centre for Health and Wellbeing, July 2004b
(http://www.wws.princeton.edu/%7Erpds/downloads/deaton_healthglobalage.pdf, accessed 1 February 2005).

Devarajan S, Miller MJ, Swanson EV. Goals for development: history, prospects and costs. Washington, DC, World Bank, 2002, Working paper no 2819 (http://econ.worldbank.org/files/13269_wps2819.pdf, accessed 1 February 2005).

Diamond J. *Guns, germs and steel: the fates of human societies.* New York, W.W. Norton, 1997.

Dicken P. *Global shift: reshaping the global economic map in the 21st century*, 4th ed. New York, Guilford Press, 2003.

Dixon R. Cancel Iraqi debt? What about Africa? *Los Angeles Times*, 26 January 2004:A3.

Dixon C, Simon D, Närman A. Introduction: The Nature of Structural Adjustment. In Simon D, van Spengen W, Dixon C, Närman A, eds., *Structurally Adjusted Africa*. London: Pluto Press: 1-14.

Dollar D, Kraay A. Growth is good for the poor, Washington, DC, World Bank, 2000, Working paper no 2587
(http://www.worldbank.org/research/growth/pdfiles/growthgoodforpoor.pdf, accessed 1 February 2005).

Dollar D. Globalization, inequality, and poverty since 1980. Washington, DC, World Bank, 2001
(http://econ.worldbank.org/files/2944_globalization-inequality-and-poverty.pdf, accessed 1 February 2005).

Dollar D. Global economic integration and global inequality. In: Gruen D, O'Brien T, Lawson J, eds. *Globalisation, living standards and inequality: recent progress and continuing challenges,* proceedings of a conference held in Sydney, 27-28 May 2002. Canberra, Reserve Bank of Australia, 2002:9-36 (http://www.rba.gov.au/PublicationsAndResearch/Conferences/2002/, accessed 1 February 2005).

Donaghu M, Barff R. Nike just did it: International subcontracting and flexibility in athletic footwear production. *Regional Studies,* 1990, 24:537-552.

Drache D, et al. One world one system? The diversity deficits in standard-setting, development and sovereignty at the WTO. Toronto, Robarts Center for Canadian Studies, York University, 2002 (Robarts Center Research Papers; http://www.yorku.ca/robarts/projects/wto/pdf/oneworldonesystem_new.pdf, accessed 1 February 2005).

Durano M. *Foreign direct investment and its impact on gender relations.* Women In Development Europe (WIDE), 2002 (http://www.eurosur.org/wide/Globalisation/IS_Durano.htm, accessed 1 February 2005).

Duxbury L, Higgins C. *Work–life conflict in Canada in the new millennium: a status report.* Ottawa, Health Canada, 2003 (http://www.phac-aspc.gc.ca/publicat/work-travail/pdf/rprt_2_e.pdf, accessed 1 February 2005).

Easterly WR. *Inequality does cause underdevelopment: new evidence.* Washington, DC, Center for Global Development, Institute for International Economics, 2002, Working Paper no. 1 (http://www.undp.org/povertycentre/publications/distribution/Easterly-InequalityDoesCauseUnderdev-CGDEV-Jun02.pdf, accessed 1 February 2005)

Ehrenreich B. *Nickel and dimed: on (not) getting by in America.* New York, Metropolitan Books, 2000.

Elliot R. Canada's new patent bill provides a basis for improvement. *Bridges Monthly Review,* 2004, 8(5):19-20.

Elliott L. Germany in search of reform. *The Guardian Weekly*, 23-29 July 2004a.

Elliott L. Deal on global trade holds out hope for poor nations. *The Guardian*, 2 August 2004b.

Elson D, Cagatay N. The social content of macroeconomic policies. *World Development*, 2000, 28(7):1347-1364.

Esping-Anderson G. *The three worlds of welfare capitalism.* Princeton, Princeton University Press, 1990.

Fligstein N, Shin TJ. The shareholder value society: a review of the changes in working conditions and inequality in the U.S., 1976-2000. Berkeley, University of California Berkeley Institute of Industrial Relations, 2003, Working Paper Series, no. iirwps-088-02 (http://repositories.cdlib.org/cgi/viewcontent.cgi?article=1026&context=iir, accessed 1 February 2005).

Focus on the Global South. *Anti poverty or anti poor? The millennium development goals and the eradication of extreme poverty and hunger.* Bangkok, 2003. (http://www.focusweb.org/pdf/MDG-2003.pdf).

Food and Agriculture Organization (FAO). *Rural women and food security: current situation and perspectives.* Rome, FAO,1996.

Frank RH, Cook PJ. *The winner-take-all society.* New York, Free Press, 1995.

Frey RS. The transfer of core-based hazardous production processes to the export processing zones of the periphery: the maquiladora centers of northern Mexico. *Journal of World-Systems Research*, 2003, 9(2):317-354.

Galeano E. *Open veins of Latin America: five centuries of the pillage of a continent.* New York, Monthly Review Press, 1973.

Galt V. Rising workloads, stress seen taking toll on productivity. *The Globe and Mail*, 29 July 2004:B6.

George S. *A fate worse than debt.* London, Penguin, 1988.

Gereffi G. International trade and international upgrading in the apparel commodity chain. *Journal of International Economics*, 1999, 48:37-70.

Gereffi G, Korzeniewicz M, eds. *Commodity chains and global capitalism.* New York, Praeger, 1994

Gershman J, Irwin A. Getting a grip on the global economy. In: Kim JY, et al., eds. *Dying for growth: global inequality and the health of the poor.* Monroe, Maine, Common Courage Press, 2000:11-43.

Global Forum for Health Research. *The 10/90 report on health research,* 2003-2004. Geneva, 2004 (http://www.globalforumhealth.org/pages/index.asp, accessed 1 February 2005).

Global Social Policy Forum. A North-South dialogue on the prospects for a socially progressive globalization. *Global Social Policy*, 2001, 1(2):147-162.

Glyn A. Social democracy and full employment. *New Left Review*, 1995, I/211(May-June):33-55.

Goldstone P. *Making the world safe for tourism.* New Haven, Yale University Press, 2001.

Goodman P, Pan P. Chinese workers pay for Wal-Mart's low prices: retailer squeezes its Asian suppliers to cut costs. *The Washington Post*, 8 February 2004:A01.

Gough I. Globalization and regional welfare regimes: the East Asian case. *Global Social Policy*, 2001, 1(2):163-190.

Greenfield G. *The WTO agreement on Trade-Related Investment Measures (TRIMS).* Canadian Center for Policy Alternatives Briefing Paper Series: Trade and Investment, 2001, 2(1):1-8.

Greenhill R, Sisti E. *Real progress report on HIPC.* London, Jubilee Research at the New Economics Foundation, 2003 (http://www.jubilee2000uk.org/analysis/reports/realprogressHIPC.pdf, accessed 1 February 2005).

Gringeri CE. Assembling 'genuine GM parts': rural homeworkers and economic development. *Economic Development Quarterly*, 1994, 8:147-157.

Groupe de travail sur les nouvelles contributions financières internationales. Rapport à M. Jacques Chirac, Président de la République (English version). Paris, Ministry of Foreign Affairs, French Republic, December 2004 (http://www.france.diplomatie.fr/actual/pdf/landau_report.pdf, accessed 17 February 2005).

Gruen D, O'Brien T, Lawson J, eds. *Globalisation, living standards and inequality: recent progress and continuing challenges,* proceedings of a conference held in Sydney, 27-28 May 2002. Canberra, Reserve Bank of Australia, 2000 (http://www.rba.gov.au/PublicationsAndResearch/Conferences/2002/, accessed 1 February 2005).

Grunberg I. Double jeopardy: globalization, liberalization and the fiscal squeeze. *World Development*, 1998, 26(4):591-605.

Gupta S, et al. Debt relief and public health spending in heavily indebted poor countries. *Bulletin of the World Health Organization*, 2002, 80(2):151-157.

Gyebi J, Brykczynska G, Lister G. Globalisation: economics and women's health, London, UK Partnership for Global Health, 2002 (http://www.ukglobalhealth.org/content/Text/Globalisation_New_version.doc, accessed 1 February 2005).

Haddad S, Mohindra K. Macroeconomic adjustment policies, health sector reform, and access, utilization and quality of health care: studying the macro-micro links. Montreal, International Development Research Centre.

Hanlon J. How much debt must be cancelled? *Journal of International Development*, 2000, 12: 877-901.

Hawley S. *Exporting corruption,* Dorset, The Corner House, 2000. (http://www.thecornerhouse.org.uk/pdf/briefing/19bribe.pdf, accessed 1 February 2005).

Held D. Globalisation: the dangers and the answers. openDemocracy.net, 27 May 2004 (http://www.opendemocracy.net/debates/article.jsp?id=6&debateId=27&articleId=1918, accessed 1 February 2005).

Henriques G, Patel R. *NAFTA, corn, and Mexico's agricultural trade liberalization.* Silver City, NM, America's Program, Interhemispheric Resource Center, 2004 (http://www.americaspolicy.org/pdf/reports/0402nafta.pdf, accessed 1 February 2005).

Higgins C, Duxbury L, Johnson K. *Exploring the link between work–life conflict and demands on Canada's health care system.* Ottawa, Public Health Agency of Canada, 2004. (http://www.phac-aspc.gc.ca/publicat/work-travail/report3/pdfs/fvwklfrprt_e.pdf, accessed 1 February 2005).

Hilary J. *The wrong model: GATS, trade liberalisation and children's right to health.* London, Save the Children, 2001 (http://www.savethechildren.org.uk/temp/scuk/cache/cmsattach/986_w rongmodel.pdf, accessed 1 February 2005).

Hilary J. *Divide and Rule: The EU and US response to developing country alliances at the WTO.* London, Action Aid International, 2004 (http://www.actionaid.org.uk/wps/content/documents/dividean-drule_0704_282004_93111.pdf, accessed 1 February 2005).

Hochschild A. Global care chains and emotional surplus value. In: Hutton W, Giddens A, eds. *Global capitalism.* New York, The New Press, 2000.

Hodess R. Introduction. In: *Global corruption report 2004.* London, Pluto Press, 2004:11-18 (http://www.globalcorruptionreport.org/ download.htm, accessed 1 February 2005) .

Howard J. Global coherence, employment and labor standards. *Global Social Policy*, 2004, 4(2):136-138.

Hughes DM. The "Natasha" trade: the transnational shadow market of trafficking in women. *Journal of International Affairs*, 2000, 53:625-651.

Human Rights Watch. *Blood, sweat and fear: workers' rights in US meat and poultry plants.* New York, Human Rights Watch, 2004 (http://www.hrw.org/reports/2005/usa0105/usa0105.pdf, accessed 21 February 2005).

Hunt P. Economic, Social and Cultural Rights: The right of everyone to the enjoyment of the highest attainable standard of physical and mental health: report of the Special Rapporteur. New York and Geneva, United Nations Economic and Social Council, 2003, document E/CN.4/2003/58 (http://www.unhchr.ch/Huridocda/Huridoca.nsf/0/9854302995c2c86fc 1256cec005a18d7/$FILE/G0310979.pdf, accessed 1 February 2005).

Hunt P. Economic, Social and Cultural Rights: The right of everyone to the enjoyment of the highest attainable standard of physical and mental health: report of the Special Rapporteur – Addendum: Mission to the World Trade Organization. New York and Geneva: United Nations Economic and Social Council, 2004, document E/CN.4/2004/49/Add.1 (http://www.unhchr.ch/huridocda/huridoca.nsf/0/5860D7D863239D82 C1256E660056432A/$File/G0411390.pdf?OpenElement, accessed 1 February 2005).

Industry Canada. An overview of Canada's trade with Africa. Ottawa, International Cooperation, International Business Branch, Industry Canada, 2002 (http://strategis.ic.gc.ca/epic/internet/inibi-iai.nsf/en/bi18682e.html, accessed 1 February 2005).

ICFTU (International Confederation of Free Trade Unions). *Export processing zones - symbols of exploitation and a development dead-end.* Brussels, ICFTU, 2003 (http://www.icftu.org/www/pdf/wtoepzre-port2003-en.pdf, accessed 1 February 2005).

International Institute for Population Sciences, ORC Macro. *National Family Health Survey (NFHS-II) 1998-99.* Mumbai, India, 2004 (http://www.nfhsindia.org/pnfhs2.html, accessed 1 February 2005).

International Labour Organization. *Labor and social issues related to export processing zones.* Geneva, ILO, 1998 (http://www.ilo.org/pub-lic/english/dialogue/govlab/legrel/tc/epz/reports/epzrepor_w61/index.h tm, accessed 1 February 2005).

International Labour Organization. *EPZ employment statistics.* Geneva, ILO, 2004a (http://www.ilo.org/public/english/dialogue/sec-tor/themes/epz/stats.htm, accessed 1 February 2005).

International Labour Organization. Definitions: What we mean when we say "economic security," Socio-Economic Security Programme fact sheet. Geneva, ILO, 2004b (http://www.ilo.org/public/english/protection/ses, accessed 1 February 2005)

International Monetary Fund. Does the IMF always prescribe fiscal austerity? Are targets too high? Transcript of an IMF book forum, Washington, DC, International Monetary Fund, June 8, 2004 (http://www.imf.org/external/np/tr/2004/tr040608.htm, accessed 1 February 2005).

Jawara F, Kwa E. *Behind the scenes at the WTO: the real world of international trade negotiations.* London, Zed Books, 2003.

Jawara F, Kwa E, Sharma S. *Behind the scenes at the WTO: the real world of international trade negotiations/lessons of Cancun, 2nd Edition.* London, Zed Books, 2004.

Jenkins, R. Globalization, production, employment and poverty: debates and evidence. *Journal of International Development*, 2004, 16:1-12.

Jeter J. The dumping ground: as Zambia courts western markets, used goods arrive at a heavy price. *The Washington Post,* 22 April 2002:A1

Junne GCA. International organizations in a period of globalization: new (problems of) legitimacy. In Coicaud JM, Heiskanen V, eds. *The legitimacy of international organizations.* Toykyo, United Nations University Press, 2001:189-220.

Kahn J, Yardley J. Amid China's boom, no helping hand for young Qingming. *New York Times Late Edition*, 1 August 2004:Section 1, Page 1. 2004.

KAIROS. Phase-out of Multi-Fibre Agreement threatens textile workers' jobs. *CCPA Monitor*, 2004, 11(3):9.

Kaplinsky R, Morris M, Readman J. The globalization of product markets and immiserizing growth: lessons from the South African furniture industry. *World Development*, 2002, 30(7):1159-1177.

Kapur D, McHale J. Migration's new payoff. *Foreign Policy*, 2003, Nov/Dec:49-58.

Karasek R, Theorell T. *Healthy work: stress, productivity and the reconstruction of working life.* New York, Basic Books, 1990.

Karl, M. *Higher agricultural education and opportunities in rural development for women.* Rome, Food and Agriculture Organization (FAO), 1997.

Kaufman L. Its prices, and its reach, push Wal-Mart to the top. *New York Times,* 2000, 22 October.

Keck A, Low P. Special and differential treatment in the WTO: why, when, and how? Geneva, World Trade Organization Economic Research and Statistics Division 2004 (Staff Working Paper ERSD-2004-03).

Kenen PB. Appraising the IMF's performance. *Finance and Development*, 2004, 41(1):41-45.

Kickbusch I, Buse K. Global influences and global responses: International Health at the turn of the 21st Century. In: Merson, MH, Black, RE, Mills, AJ, eds. *Handbook of International Public Health.* Aspen Publishers, 2001:701-737.

Killick T. Politics, evidence and the new aid agenda. *Development Policy Review*, 2004, 22(1):5-29.

Kim JY, et al., eds. *Dying for growth: global inequality and the health of the poor.* Monroe, Maine, Common Courage Press, 2000.

Knappe M. Textile and clothing: what happens after 2005? *International Trade Forum*, 2003, 2:16.

Labonte R. Globalism and health: threats and opportunities. *Health Promotion Journal of Australia*, 1999, 9(2):126-132.

Labonte R, Schrecker T. Committed to health for all? how the G7/G8 rate. *Social Science and Medicine*, 2004, 59:1661-1676.

Labonte R, Schrecker T, Sanders D, Meeus W. *Fatal indifference: the G8, Africa and global health.* Cape Town, University of Cape Town Press, 2004.

Labonte R, Schrecker T, Sen Gupta A. A global health equity agenda for the G8 summit. *British Medical Journal* 330, 2005, 330-336.

Labonte R, Schrecker T. *The G8, Africa and global health: a platform for global health equity for the 2005 summit.* London, Nuffield Trust, in press, (to be available at http://www.nuffieldtrust.org.uk).

Labonte R, Torgerson R. *A Critical Review of Frameworks Linking Globalization and Health*, STU/H&T/2003.2. Geneva, World Health Organization, 2003.

LaFraniere S. Donor mistrust worsens AIDS in Zimbabwe. *New York Times.* 12 August, 2004.

Lambo E, Sambo L. Health sector reform in Sub-Saharan Africa: a synthesis of country experiences. *East African Medical Journal*, 2003, 80(6):S1-S20.

Lang T. Food Industrialisation and Food Power: Implications for Food Governance. *Development Policy Review*, 2003, 21: 555-568.

Leclerc-Madlala S. Infect one, infect all: Zulu youth response to the AIDS epidemic in South Africa. *Medical Anthropology*, 1997, 77:363-380.

Lee K. The global dimensions of cholera. *Global Change and Human Health*, 2001, 4(1):6-17.

Leon F. The case of the Chilean health system, 1983-2000. In: Vieira C, Drager N, eds. *Trade in health services: global, regional and country perspectives.* Washington, DC, Pan American Health Organization, 2002.

Levine DI. *Reinventing the workplace.* Washington, DC, The Brookings Institution, 1995.

Lewis JD, Robinson S, Thierfelder K. Free trade agreements and the SADC economies. *Journal of African Economies*, 2003, 12(2):156-206.

Lichfield G. Mexico: Revolution ends, change begins (Survey). *The Economist*, 28 October 2000.

Lindsey B. Do cheap imports hurt poor countries? 2002. (http://www.brinklindsey.com/archives/2002_04.php, accessed 1 February 2005).

Lissakers K. Blunt approach does the trick. *Finance and Development*, 2004, 41(1):46-47.

Lister G, Ingram A, Prowle, M. Country case study: UK financing of international cooperation for health. New York, Office of Development Studies, United Nations Development Programme, 2004 (http://www.sti.ch/pdfs/swap385.pdf, accessed1 February 2005).

Liu Y et al. China: increasing health gaps in a transitional economy. In: Whitehead M, et al., eds. *Challenging inequities in health: from ethics to action.* New York, Oxford University Press, 2001:76-89.

Liu Y, Rao K, Hsiao WC. Medical expenditure and rural impoverishment in China. *Journal of Health, Population and Nutrition*, 2003, 21(3):216-222.

Loftus AJ, McDonald DA. Of liquid dreams: a political ecology of water privatization in Buenos Aires. *Environment & Urbanization*, 2001, 13(2):179-200.

Lozano R, et al. Mexico: marginality, need, and resource allocation at the county level. In: Whitehead M, et al., eds. *Challenging inequities in health: from ethics to action.* New York, Oxford University Press, 2001:276-295.

MacAskill E. Aim is to meet UN target by 2013. *The Guardian*, 13 July 2004.

Mackay J, Ericksen M. *The Tobacco Atlas.* Geneva: World Health Organziation, 2002 (http://www.who.int/tobacco/statistics/tobacco_atlas/en/, accessed1 February 2005).

Mahdavi S. Shifts in the composition of government spending in response to external debt burden. *World Development*, 2004, 32(7):1139-1157.

Manda DK, Sen K. The labor market effects of globalization in Kenya. *Journal of International Development*, 2004, 16:29-43.

Marchak P. *The integrated circus: the new right and the restructuring of global markets.* Montreal, McGill-Queen's University Press, 1991.

Martin M. Assessing the HIPC initiative: the key policy debates. In: Teunissen J, Akkerman A, eds. HIPC debt relief: myths and realities. The Hague, *Forum on Debt and Development (FONDAD),* 2004:11-47.

Martineau T, Decker K, Bundred P. "Brain drain" of health professionals: from rhetoric to responsible action. *Health Policy,* 2004, 70:1-10.

Mavrotas G. *The UK HM Treasury – DFID proposal to increase external finance to developing countries: the international finance facility.* Helsinki, United Nations University World Institute Development Economics Research (UNU/WIDER), 2003 (WIDER Conference on Sharing Global Prosperity, Helsinki, 6-7 September, 2003; http://www.wider.unu.edu/conference/conference-2003-3/ conference-2003-3-papers/IFFpaper-Final_new_-mavrotas.pdf, accessed 1 February 2005).

McCubbins T. Somebody kicked the sleeping dog: new bite in the Foreign Corrupt Practices Act. *Business Horizons,* 2001, January/February:27-32.

McDonald D. No money, no service: South Africa's poorest citizens lose out under attempts to recover service costs for water and power. *Alternatives Journal,* 2002, 28(2):16-20.

McIntosh A. The poor pay more for their water. *Habitat Debate,* 2003, 9(3):12 (http://www.unhabitat.org/hd/hdv9n3/12.asp, accessed 21 February 2005).

McIntyre T, Nguyen TD. Corporate Income Taxes in the Bush Years. Washington, DC, Citizens for Tax Justice, September 2004 (http://www.ctj.org/corpfed04an.pdf, accessed 1 February 2005).

Mead WR. Bushism found: a second-term agenda hidden in trade agreements. *Harper's Magazine,* 1992, September:37-45.

Michaud C. Development assistance for health (DAH): recent trends and resource allocation. Geneva, World Health Organization, 2003, paper prepared for second consultation, Commission on Macroeconomics and Health, October 29-30, 2003. Geneva, WHO (http://www.who.int/macrohealth/events/health_for_poor/en/dah_trends_nov10.pdf, accessed 1 February 2005).

Milanovic B. The two faces of globalization: against globalization as we know it. *World Development*, 2003, 31(4):667-683.

Milberg W. 2004. The changing structure of international trade linked to global production systems: what are the policy implications? Working Paper No. 33. Geneva: World Commission on the Social Dimensions of Globalization, International Labour Office (http://www.ilo.org/public/english/bureau/integration/download/publicat/4_3_247_wcsdg-wp-33.pdf, accessed 1 February 2005).

Milward B. What is structural adjustment? In: Mohan G, et al. eds. *Structural adjustment: theory, practice and impacts.* London, Routledge, 2000:24-38.

Minujin A, Delamonica E. Mind the gap! Widening child mortality disparities. *Journal of Human Development*, 2003, 4(3):397-418.

Mishel L, Bernstein J, Allegretto S. The state of working America 2004/2005, Washington, DC, *Economic Policy Institute*, 2004.

Monbiot G. *The Age of Consent: a manifesto for a new world order.* London, Perennial, 2003.

Mtonga CQ, Chikoti S. Zambia country paper on textiles and clothing. Lusaka, Ministry of Commerce Trade and Industry, Government of Zambia, 2002 (http://www.intracen.org/worldtradenet/docs/whatsnew/atc_lesotho_november2002/country_paper_zambia.pdf, accessed 1 February 2005).

Mumtaz Z, et al. Gender-based barriers to primary health care provision in Pakistan: the experience of female providers. *Health Policy and Planning*, 2003, 18(3):261-269.

Murray R, ed. *Multinationals beyond the market: intra-firm trade and the control of transfer pricing.* New York, Wiley, 1981.

Mustard CA et al. Paying Taxes and Using Health Care Services:The Distributional Consequences of Tax Financed Universal Health Insurance in a Canadian Province, paper presented to the Conference on the State of Living Standards and the Quality of Life in Canada. Ottawa, Centre for the Study of Living Standards, October 30-31, 1998 (http://www.csls.ca/events/oct98/must1.pdf, accessed 1 February 2005).

Muuka GN. Zambia's SAP - a response to Sam Okoroafo's paper: "Managerial perceptions of the impact of economic reform measures on the economic reforms and firm performance in restructuring economies: a comparative assessment." *The Journal of Business in Developing Nations*, 1997, 1.

Nantulya VM et al, eds. Road traffic injuries and health equity (special issue). *Injury Control and Safety Promotion*, 2003, 10(1-2).

Naylor RT. *Hot Money: Peekaboo Finance and the Politics of Debt.* Toronto, McClelland & Stewart, 1987.

Ndikumana L, Boyce JK. Public debts and private assets: explaining capital flight from sub-Saharan African countries. *World Development*, 2003, 31(1):107-130.

Nelson PJ, Dorsey E. At the nexus of human rights and development: new methods and strategies of global NGOs. *World Development*, 2003, 31(12): 2013-2026.

Nelson SH. The West's moral obligation to assist developing nations in the fight against HIV/AIDS. *Health Care Analysis*, 2002, 10:87-108.

Norton-Taylor R, White M, Hencke D. Tanzania cash for BAE system on hold pending inquiry. *The Guardian*, March 21 2002.

Nygren-Krug H. *25 questions & answers on health & human rights.* Geneva, World Health Organization, 2002 (http://www.who.int/hhr/information/25%20Questions%20and%20An swers%20on%20Health%20and%20Human%20Rights.pdf, accessed 1 February 2005).

O'Brien R. Organizational Politics, Multilateral Economic Organizations and Social Policy. *Global Social Policy*, 2002, 2: 141-162.

Okoroafo SC. Managerial perceptions of the impact of economic reform measures on the economic environment reforms and firm performance in restructuring economies: a comparative assessment. *Journal of Business in Developing Nations*, 1997, 1.

Oloka-Onyango J, Udugama D. *Economic, Social and Cultural Rights: Globalization and its impact on the full enjoyment of human rights, Final Report.* Geneva: United Nations Economic and Social Council, 2003, document E/CN.4/Sub.2/2003/14 (http://www.unhchr.ch/, accessed 1 February 2005).

O'Manique C. *Neoliberalism and AIDS crisis in sub-Saharan Africa: globalization's pandemic.* Houndmills, UK, Palgrave Macmillan, 2004.

Orbinski J. Access to medicines and global health: will Canada lead or flounder? *Canadian Medical Association Journal*, 2004, 170:224-226.

Organization for Economic Cooperation and Development (OECD). Public social expenditure by main category as a percentage of GDP (1980-1998). Paris, 2004a (http://www.oecd.org/dataoecd/43/14/2087083.xls, accessed 1 February 2005).

Organization for Economic Cooperation and Development (OECD) Development Assistance Committee. Development co-operation: 2003 report. *DAC Journal,* 2004b, 5(1) [full issue].

Organization for Economic Cooperation and Development (OECD) Development Assistance Committee. Development co-operation: 2004 report, *DAC Journal 2005,* 6(1)[full issue].

Otsuki T, Wilson J, Sewadeh M. A Race to the Top? A Case Study of Food Safety Standards and African Exports. Washington, DC, World Bank, 2001 (http://econ.worldbank.org/files/1424_wps2563.pdf, accessed 1 February 2005).

Oxfam International. *G8: failing the world's children.* Washington, DC, 2001.

Oxfam America. *Debt relief: good enough for Iraq, why not Africa?* Washington, DC. 2004 (http://www.oxfamamerica.org/newsandpublications/press_releases/art7329.html, accessed 1 February 2005).

Ozoemena C. Atiku in London, in search of stolen wealth. *Vanguard* (Lagos), 2004, 22 August.

Parkhurst JO, Lush L. The political environment of HIV: lessons from a comparison of Uganda and South Africa. *Social Science and Medicine*, 2004, 59:1913-1924.

Patnaik U. *The republic of hunger.* New Delhi, Economic Research Foundation, 2004 (http://www.networkideas.org/featart/apr2004/Republic_Hunger.pdf, accessed 1 February 2005).

Pettifor A, Greenhill R. *Debt relief and the millennium development goals.* New York, United Nations Development Programme, 2002 (http://hdr.undp.org/docs/publications/background_papers/2003/HDR2 003_Pettifor_Greenhill.pdf, accessed 1 February 2005)

Polanyi M, Tompa E, Foley, J. Labor market flexibility and worker insecurity. In: Raphael, D, ed. *Social determinants of health. Canadian perspectives*. Toronto, Canadian Scholars' Press, 2004:67-77.

Pollock AM, Price D. New deal from the World Trade Organisation ... may not provide essential medicines for poor countries. *British Medical Journal,* 2003, 327:571-572.

Prasad E, et al. *Effects of financial globalization on developing countries: some empirical evidence.* Washington, DC, International Monetary Fund, 2003 (http://www.imf.org/external/np/res/docs/2003/031703.pdf, accessed 1 February 2005).

Preibisch KL, Rivera Herrejon G, Wiggins SL. Defending food security in a free-market economy: the gendered dimensions of restructuring in rural Mexico. *Human Organization*, 2002, 61(1):68-79.

Quinlan M, Mayhew C, Bohle P. The global expansion of precarious employment, work disorganization, and consequences for occupational health: placing the debate in a comparative historical context. *International Journal of Health Services*, 2001, 31(3):507-536.

Ramo JC. *The Beijing consensus.* London, The Foreign Policy Center, 2004 (http://www.fpc.org.uk/fsblob/240.pdf, accessed 1 February 2005).

Ravallion M. *Competing concepts of inequality in the globalization debate.* Washington, DC, The World Bank, 2004 (http://econ.world-bank.org/files/34170_wps3243.pdf, accessed 1 February 2005).

Reddy SG, Pogge TW. *How not to count the poor.* New York, Columbia University, New York, 2003 (version 4.5; http://www.columbia.edu/~sr793/count.pdf, accessed 1 February 2005).

Reich R. *The work of nations: preparing ourselves for 21st Century capitalism.* New York, Vintage, 1992.

Reinicke W. *Global public policy: governing without government?* Washington, DC, Brookings Institute, 1998.

Rice J, Prince M. *Changing politics of Canadian social policy.* Toronto, University of Toronto Press, 2000.

Rich B. *Mortgaging the earth: the World Bank, environmental impoverishment and the crisis of development.* Boston, Beacon Press, 1994.

Richard AO. International trafficking in women to the United States: a contemporary manifestation of slavery and organized crime. Washington, DC, US Central Intelligence Agency, 2000 (DCI exceptional intelligence analyst program intelligence monograph (www.cia.gov/csi/monograph/women/trafficking.pdf, accessed 1 February 2005).

Richter J. *Holding corporations accountable.* London, Zed Books, 2001.

Ringen K. Edwin Chadwick, the market ideology and sanitary reform. On the nature of the 19th centruy public health movement. *International Journal of Health Services*, 1979, 9(1):107-120.

Rodriguez F, Rodrik D. *Trade Policy and Economic Growth: A Skeptic's Guide to the Cross-National Evidence, Discussion Paper 2143.* London, Centre for Economic Policy Research, 2000 (http://ksghome.harvard.edu/~drodrik/skepti1299.pdf, accessed 1 February 2005).

Rodrik D. *The New Global Economy and Developing Countries: Making Openness Work.* Baltimore, Johns Hopkins University Press, 1999.

Rodrik D. *The Global Governance of Trade as if Development Really Mattered.* New York, Bureau for Development Policy, United Nations Development Programme, October 2001 (http://www.undp.org/main-undp/propoor/docs/pov_globalgovernancetrade_pub.pdf, accessed 1 February 2005).

Rogerson A, Hewitt A, Waldenberg D. *The international aid system 2005-2010: forces for and against change.* London, Overseas Development Institute, 2004 (Working Paper 235; http://www.odi.org.uk/publications/working_papers/wp235.pdf, accessed 1 February 2005).

Rowson M, Verheul E. Pushing the boundaries: health and the next round of PRSPs. Amsterdam, WEMOS, 2004 (http://medact.org/content/Wemos%20and%20Medact%20-%20Pushing%20the%20boundaries.pdf, accessed 1 February 2005-).

Rugman AM, Verbeke A. The World Trade Organization, multinational enterprise, and civil society. In: Fratianni M, Savona P, Kirton J, eds., *Sustaining global growth and development: G7 and IMF governance.* Aldershot, Ashgate Publishing Co., 2003:81-97.

Sachs JD, Gallop JL. The economic burden of malaria. Geneva, World Health Organization Commision on Macroeconomics and Health, 2001 (CMH Working Paper Series, no. WG1:10; http://www.cmhealth.org/docs/wg1_paper10.pdf, accessed 1 February 2005).

Sachs JD, et al. Ending Africa's poverty trap. *Brookings Papers on Economic Activity*, 2004, no. 1:117-240.

Sanger M. *Reckless abandon: Canada, the GATS and the future of health care.* Ottawa, Canadian Center for Policy Alternatives, 2001.

Sanger M, Sinclair S., eds. *Putting health first: Canadian health care reform in a globalizing world.* Ottawa, Canadian Centre for Policy Alternatives, 2004.

Satterthwaite D. The millennium development goals and urban poverty reduction: great expectations and nonsense statistics. *Environment & Urbanization*, 2003, 15:181-190.

Schoepf BG. Inscribing the body politic: AIDS in Africa. In: Lock M, Kaufert P, eds. *Pragmatic women and body politics*. Cambridge, Cambridge University Press, 1998:98-126.

Schoepf BG, Schoepf C, Millen JV. Theoretical therapies, remote remedies: SAPs and the political ecology of poverty and health in Africa. In: Kim JY, et al., eds. *Dying for growth: global inequality and the health of the poor*. Monroe, Maine, Common Courage Press, 2000:91-126.

Schrecker T, Labonte R. Taming the brain drain : a challenge for public health systems in southern Africa. *International Journal of Occupational and Environmental Health*, 2004, 10:409-415.

Schreuder B, Kostermans C. Global health strategies versus local primary health care priorities - a case study of national immunisation days in southern Africa. *South African Medical Journal*, 2001, 91(3):249-254.

Schwartz MJ. Discussion. In: Gruen D, O'Brien T, Lawson J, eds. *Globalisation, living standards and inequality: recent progress and continuing challenges,* proceedings of a conference held in Sydney, 27-28 May 2002. Canberra, Reserve Bank of Australia, 2002:147-178 (http://www.rba.gov.au/PublicationsAndResearch/Conferences/2002/ , accessed 1 February 2005).

SEATINI (Southern and Eastern African Trade and Information Negotiations Initiative), EQUINET (Southern African Regional Network for Equity in Health (EQUINET). *The WTO Global Agreement on Trade in Services (GATS) and Health Equity in Southern Africa,* Equinet Policy Series No. 12. Harare, EQUINET (http://www.equinetafrica.org/bibl/docs/POL12trade%20.pdf, accessed 1 February 2005).

Sell SK. *Private power, public law: the globalization of intellectual property rights.* Cambridge, Cambridge University Press, 2003.

Sen A. Freedom's market. *The Observer*, 25 June 2000.

Sen A, Himanshu. *Poverty and inequality in India.* New Delhi, Economic Research Foundation, 2004 (http://www.networkideas.org/featart/may2004/Poverty_WC.pdf, accessed 1 February 2005).

Sen K, Bonita R. Global health status: two steps forward, one step back. *The Lancet,* 2000, 356(9229):577-582.

Serafini J. Foreign Corrupt Practices Act. (Survey of white collar crime). *American Criminal Law Review*, 2004, 41:721-750.

Sexton S. *Trading health care away? GATS, public services and privatization,* Dorset, The Corner House, 2001 (http://www.thecorner-house.org.uk/pdf/briefing/23gats.pdf, accessed 1 February 2005).

Shaffer E, Brenner JE, Yamin A. Comments regarding the Free Trade Area of the Americas negotiations: effects on universal access to health care and water services. San Francisco, The Center for Policy Analysis on Trade and Health (CPATH), 2002 (http://www.tradeobser-vatory.org/library.cfm?refID=25632, accessed 1 February 2005).

Shrybman S. A legal opinion concerning water export controls and Canadian obligations under NAFTA and the WTO. Vancouver, West Coast Environmental Law, 1999 (http://www.wcel.org/wcelpub/1999/12926.html, accessed 1 February 2005).

Sinclair S. *GATS: how the World Trade Organization's new "services" negotiations threaten democracy.* Ottawa, Canadian Center for Policy Alternatives, 2000.

Sinclair S. *NAFTA Chapter 11 Investor-State Disputes.* Ottawa, Canadian Center for Policy Alternatives, 2005 (http://www.policyal-ternatives.ca. accessed 15 January 2005).

Singer M. Engaging emergent diseases and emergent causes of disease. *Anthropology News*, 2004, 44(6).

Smeeding TM. Globalisation, inequality and the rich countries of the G-20: evidence from the Luxembourg Income Study (LIS). In: Gruen D, O'Brien T, Lawson J, eds. *Globalisation, living standards and inequality: recent progress and continuing challenges,* proceedings of a conference held in Sydney, 27-28 May 2002. Canberra, Reserve Bank of Australia, 2002:179-206 (http://www.rba.gov.au/PublicationsAndResearch/Conferences/2002/ , accessed 1 February 2005).

Social Watch. *Fear and want: obstacles to human security, Social Watch Report 2004.* Montevideo, Uruguay, 2004 (http://www.social-watch.org/en/informeImpreso/index.htm#, accessed 1 February 2005).

Solt F. *Economic inequality and democratic political engagement.* Houston, Rice University, 2004 (http://www.unc.edu/~fredsolt/papers/Solt2004MPSA.pdf, accessed 1 February 2005).

Sparr P. What is structural adjustment? In: Sparr P, ed. *Mortgaging women's lives: feminist critiques of structural adjustment.* London, Zed Books, 2000:1-12.

Srivastava S, Theodore N. *America's High Tech Bust: Report to the Washington Alliance of Technology Workers, Communications Workers of America, Local 37083.* Chicago, Center for Urban Economic Development, University of Illinois at Chicago, September 2004 (http://www.uic.edu/cuppa/uicued/AmericasHighTechBust.pdf, accessed 1 February 2005).

Statistics Canada. *The Canadian labour market at a glance: 2003.* Ottawa, Labour Statistics Division, Statistics Canada, 2004 (Catalogue no. 71-222-XIE). (http://www.statcan.ca/english/freepub/71-222-XIE/71-222-XIE2004000.pdf, accessed 1 February 2005).

Stiglitz J. *Globalization and its discontents.* New York, W.W. Norton, 2003.

Stoppard A. *Corporate bribery on the rise worldwide.* New York, Global Policy Forum, 2002 (http://www.globalpolicy.org/nations/corrupt/2002/0514rise.htm, accessed 1 February 2005).

Strange S. *Casino capitalism*. Oxford, Blackwell, 1986.

Strange S. The new world of debt. *New Left Review*, 1998, 230:91-114.

Suh KN, Kain KC, Keystone JS. Malaria. *Canadian Medical Association Journal*, 2004, 170(11):1693-1701.

Sullivan R. A novel private sector initiative for the poor. *Habitat Debate*, 2003, 9(3):16.

Sullivan T, Shainblum E. Trading in health: the World Trade Organization (WTO) and the international regulation of health and safety. *Health Law in Canada*, 2001, 22(2):29-47.

Sullivan TA, Warren E, Westbrook JL. *The fragile middle class: Americans in debt*. New Haven, Yale University Press, 2000.

Szreter S. Rapid economic growth and 'the four Ds' of disruption, deprivation, disease and death: public health lessons from nineteenth-century Britain for twenty-first-century China? *Tropical Medicine and International Health*, 1999, 4: 146-152.

The Center for Public Integrity. *The water barons: promoting privatization*. Washington, DC, The Center for Public Integrity, 3 February 2003 (http://www.publicintegrity.org/water/report.aspx?aid=45, accessed 1 February 2005).

't Hoen E. TRIPS, pharmaceutical patents and access to essential medicines: a long way from Seattle to Doha. *Chicago Journal of International Law*, 2002, 3:27-46.

Tibaijuka A. The cost of differential gender roles in Africa agriculture: a case study of smallholder banana-coffee farms in Kagera Region. *Journal of Agricultural Economics*, 1994, 45(1):69-81.

Tourigny S, Jones-Brown D, In the aftermath of welfare 'reform'. *Social Justice*, 28(4), 2001 [special issue].

Tuckman J. Mexicans turn to pawn shops for survival. *The Guardian Weekly*, 3-9 September, 2004:18.

Ugarte MB, Zarate L, Farley M. Prostitution and trafficking of women and children from Mexico to the United States. In: Farley M, ed. *Prostitution, trafficking, and traumatic stress*. New York, Haworth Maltreatment & Trauma Press, 2003:147-165.

UN Millennium Project. *Investing in development: a practical plan to achieve the Millennium Development Goals.* London: Earthscan, 2005 (http://unmp.forumone.com/eng_full_report/TF1mainreportComplete-highres.pdf, accessed 1 February 2005).

UNRISD. *Visible Hands: Taking Responsibility for Social Development.* Geneva: United Nations Research Institute for Social Development, 2000.

United Nations Conference on Trade and Development (UNCTAD). *Globalization and liberalization: effects of international economic relations on poverty.* New York and Geneva, 1996.

United Nations Conference on Trade and Development (UNCTAD). *Trade and development report 1999: fragile recovery and risks, trade, finance and growth.* New York and Geneva, United Nations, 1999 (http://www.unctad.org/en/docs/tdr1999_en.pdf, accessed 1 February 2005).

United Nations Conference on Trade and Development (UNCTAD). *Prospects for foreign direct investment and the strategies of transnational corporations, 2004-2007.* New York, 2004a (http://www.unctad.org/en/docs/iteiit20048_en.pdf, accessed 1 February 2005).

United Nations Conference on Trade and Development (UNCTAD). *Economic development in Africa: debt sustainability: oasis or mirage?* New York, United Nations, 2004b (http://www.unctad.org/en/docs/iteiit20048_en.pdf, accessed 1 February 2005).

United Nations Development Programme. *Human development report 1999: globalization with a human face.* New York, Oxford University Press, New York, 1999. (http://hdr.undp.org/reports/global/1999/en/pdf/hdr_1999_full.pdf, accessed 1 February 2005).

United Nations Development Programme. *Human development report 2003: millennium development goals: a compact among nations to end human poverty.* New York, Oxford University Press, 2003 (http://hdr.undp.org/reports/global/2003/pdf/hdr03_complete.pdf, accessed 1 February 2005).

United Nations Environment Programme. *Global environmental outlook 2000*, London, UNEP Earthscan, 1999 (http://www.unep.org/geo2000/english/index.htm, accessed 1 February 2005).

United Nations Environment Programme. *UNEP 2000 annual report.* Nairobi, 2000. (http://www.unep.org/Evaluation/Reports/2000/, accessed 1 February 2005).

United Nations Food and Agriculture Organization. *The state of food insecurity in the world 2003*. Rome, 2003. (http://www.fao.org/documents/show_cdr.asp?url_file=/docrep/006/j0083e/j0083e00.htm, accessed 1 February 2005).

United Nations Human Settlements Programme (UN-HABITAT). *State of the world's cities: trends in Latin America and the Caribbean. Nairobi*, UN-HABITAT, 2003a (http://www.unhabitat.org/mediacentre/documents/sowc/RegionalLAC.pdf, accessed 1 February 2005).

United Nations Human Settlements Programe (UN-HABITAT). *Slums of the world: the face of urban poverty in the new millennium?* Nairobi, UN Habitat, 2003b. (http://www.unhabitat.org/publication/slumreport.pdf, accessed 1 February 2005).

United Nations Secretary-General. *Outcome of the International Conference on Financing for Development.* New York, United Nations, 2002 (Report no. A/57/344; http://www.un.org/esa/ffd/a57-344-ffd-outcome.pdf, accessed 1 February 2005).

United Nations System Standing Committee on Nutrition. *5th report on the world nutrition situation: nutrition for improved development outcomes.* New York and Geneva, United Nations, 2004 (http://www.unsystem.org/scn/Publications/AnnualMeeting/SCN31/SCN5Report.pdf, accessed 1 February 2005).

US Department of Commerce. *Addressing the challenges of international bribery and fair competition.* Washington, DC: International Trade Administration, US Department of Commerce, 2004 (Sixth Annual Report Under Section 6 of the International Anti-Bribery and Fair Competition Act of 1998, July (http://www.tcc.mac.doc.gov/pdf/2004bribery.pdf, accessed 1 February 2005).

Vasagar J. EU freezes $150m to aid 'corrupt' Kenya. *The Guardian Weekly*, 30 July - 5 August 2004:10.

Wade RH. Globalisation, poverty and income distribution: does the liberal argument hold? In: Gruen D, O'Brien T, Lawson J, eds. *Globalisation, living standards and inequality: recent progress and continuing challenges,* proceedings of a conference held in Sydney, 27-28 May 2002. Canberra, Reserve Bank of Australia, 2002:37-65 (http://www.rba.gov.au/PublicationsAndResearch/Conferences/2002/ , accessed 1 February 2005).

Wade RH. Bridging the digital divide: new route to development or new form of dependency. *Global Governance*, 2003, 8:443-466.

Wade RH. Is globalization reducing poverty and inequality? *World Development*, 2004, 32(4):567-589.

Wagstaff A, et al. *The millennium development goals for health: rising to the challenges.* Washington, DC, World Bank, 2003 (http://www-wds.worldbank.org/servlet/WDSContentServer/WDSP/IB/2004/07/15/000009486_20040715130626/Rendered/PDF/296730PAPER0Mi1ent0goals0for0health.pdf, accessed 1 February 2005).

Walt G. Globalisation of international health. *The Lancet*, 1998, 351:434-437.

Walton J, Seddon D. *Free Markets and Food Riots: The Politics of Global Adjustment.* Cambridge, MA, Blackwell, 1994.

Wasserman E, Cornejo S. Trade in health services in the region of the Americas. In: Vieira C, Drager N, eds. *Trade in health services: global, regional and country perspectives.* Washington DC, Pan American Health Organization, 2002.

Watkins K. Making globalization work for the poor. *Finance & Development*, 2002, 39(1).

Weatherspoon DD, Reardon T. The rise of supermarkets in Africa: implications for agrifood systems and the rural poor. *Development Policy Review*, 2003, 21:333-355.

Webby RJ, Webster RG. Are we ready for pandemic influenza? *Science*, 2003, 302:1519-1523.

Weisbrot M, et al. *The scorecard on globalization 1980-2000: twenty years of diminished progress*. Washington, DC, CEPR: Center for Economic and Policy Research, 2001.

Weisman J. US firms keep billions overseas: Kerry's plan spotlights huge untaxed earnings. *The Washington Post*, 2 April 2004:A01.

Welch C. Credible start, untested impact. *Finance and Development,* 2004, 41(1):50-51.

White H, Killick T. *African poverty at the millennium: causes, complexities, and challenges.* Washington, DC, The International Bank for Reconstruction and Development/The World Bank, 2001.

Williamson J. *Winners and losers over two centuries of globalization.* Helsinki, United Nations University World Institute for Development Economics Research (UNU/WIDER), 2002 (WIDER Annual Lecture 6; http://www.nber.org/papers/w9161.pdf, accessed 1 February 2005).

Williamson J. What Washington means by policy reform. In J. Williamson, ed., *Latin American Adjustment: How Much Has Happened?* Washington, DC, Institute for International Economics, 1990: 7-38.

Williamson J. *The Washington Consensus as policy prescription for development.* Washington, DC, World Bank, 2004 (World Bank Practitioners for Development lecture, 13 January; http://www.iie.com/publications/papers/williamson0204.pdf, accessed 1 February 2005).

Witte G. As income gap widens, uncertainty spreads: more US families struggle to stay on track. *The Washington Post,* 20 September 2004:A01.

Wiwa K. Money for nothing - and the debt is for free. *The Globe and Mail,* 22 May 2004:A19.

Wojcicki JM, Malala J. Condom use, power and HIV/AIDS risk:sex-workers bargain for survival in Hillbrow/Joubert Park/Berea, Johannesburg. *Social Science and Medicine,* 2001,53:99-121.

Wojcicki JM. "She drank his money:" survival sex and the problem of violence in taverns in Gauteng Province, South Africa. *Medical Anthropology Quarterly*, 2002, 16:267-293.

Woodward D. Effects of globalization and liberalization on poverty: concepts and issues. In: United Nations Conference on Trade and Development, ed. *Globalization and liberalization: effects of international economic relations on poverty*. New York and Geneva, UNCTAD, 1996.

Woodward D, Drager N, Beaglehole R, & Lipson D. Globalization and health: A framework for analysis and action. *Bulletin of the World Health Organization*, 2001, 79: 875-881.

World Bank. *World development report 1993: investing in health*. New York, Oxford University Press, 1993.

World Bank. *World development report 1995: workers in an integrating world*. New York, Oxford University Press, 1995.

World Bank. *Briefing note to the board: costing the sevice delivery MDGs: primary education, health & water supply and sanitation.* Washington, DC, 2003 (http://www-wds.worldbank.org/servlet/WDSContentServer/WDSP/IB/2003/04/25/000094946_03041604014621/Rendered/PDF/multi0page.pdf, accessed 1 February 2005.

World Bank. *World development indicators 2004*. Washington, DC, World Bank, 2004.

World Bank/International Monetary Fund. *Market Access for Developing Country Exports - Selected Issues*. Washington, DC, Internatoinal Monteary Fund, September 26, 2002 (http://www.imf.org/external/np/pdr/ma/2002/eng/092602.pdf, accessed 1 February 2005).

World Commission on Environment and Development. *Our common future*. New York, Oxford University Press, 1987.

World Commision on the Social Dimension of Globalization. *A fair globalization: creating opportunities for all. Geneva, International Labor Organization, 2004* (http://www.ilo.org/public/english/wcsdg/docs/report.pdf, accessed 1 February 2005).

World Health Organization. *World health report 2000: Healths Systems: improving performance.* Geneva, World Health Organization, 2000 (http://www.who.int/whr/2000/en/whr00_en.pdf, accessed 1 February 2005).

World Health Organization. *World health report 2003: shaping the future.* Geneva, World Health Organization, 2003 (http://www.who.int/whr/2003/en/whr03_en.pdf, accessed 1 February 2005).

World Health Organization. *World health report 2004: changing history.* Geneva, World Health Organization, 2004 (http://www.who.int/whr/2004/en/report04_en.pdf, accessed 1 February 2005).

World Social Forum. *World Social Forum charter of principles.* Mumbai, World Social Forum, 2001 (http://www.wsfindia.org/charter.php, accessed 1 February 2005).

World Trade Organization. *Zambia's economic and trade reforms start to show benefits.* Geneva, World Trade Organization, 1996 (http://www.wto.org/english/tratop_e/tpr_e/tp37_e.htm, accessed 1 February 2005).

World Trade Organization. *European communities-measures affecting asbestos and asbestos containing products: report of the panel.* Geneva, World Trade Organization, 2000 (http://www.worldtradelaw.net/reports/wtoab/ec-asbestos(ab).pdf, accessed 1 February 2005).

World Trade Organization. *Declaration on the TRIPS agreement and public health.* Doha, Ministerial Conference, 4th Session (document WT/MIN(01)/DEC/2). Geneva, World Trade Organization, 2001a. (http://www.wto.org/english/thewto_e/minist_e/min01_e/mindecl_trips_e.pdf, accessed 1 February 2005).

World Trade Organization. *Doha decision on implementation-related decisions and concerns.* Doha, Ministerial Conference, 4th Session (document WT/MIN(01)/17). Geneva, World Trade Organization, 2001b (http://www.wto.org/english/thewto_e/minist_e/min01_e/mindecl_implementation_e.pdf, accessed 1 February 2005).

World Trade Organization. *Doha ministerial declaration.* Doha, Ministerial Conference, 4th Session (document WT/MIN(01)/DEC/1). Geneva, World Trade Organization, 2001c (http://www.wto.org/english/thewto_e/minist_e/min01_e/mindecl_e.pdf, accessed 1 February 2005).

WTO Services Database Online, http://tsdb.wto.org/wto/, accessed 24 November, 2002.

World Trade Organization. *Implementation of paragraph 6 of the Doha Declaration on the TRIPS agreement and public health, decision of the General Council of 30 August 2003.* Geneva, World Trade Organization, 2003 (http://www.wto.org/english/tratop_e/trips_e/implem_para6_e.htm, accessed 1 February 2005).

Worldwatch Institute. *Vital Signs 2001,* New York: W.W. Norton and Co., 2001.

Wysocki B. The outlook: foreigners find U.S. a good place to invest. *The Wall Street Journal,* 7 August 1995.

Yach D. Chronic Disease and Disability of the Poor: Tackling the Challenge. *Development,* 2001, 44(1):59-65.

Yunker JA. Could a global Marshall Plan be successful? An investigation using the WEEP simulation model. *World Development,* 2004, 32(7):1109-1137.

Zarrilli S. The case of Brazil. In: Vieira C, Drager N, eds. *Trade in health services: global, regional and country perspectives.* Washington, DC, Pan American Health Organization, 2002.